Inside
LOG HOMES
THE ART AND SPIRIT
OF HOME DÉCOR

The Art & Spirit of Home Décor

Inside
LOG HOMES

CINDY THIEDE

Photographs by Jonathan Stoke & Cindy Thiede

Gibbs Smith, Publisher
Salt Lake City

09 08 07   7 6 5 4

Published by
Gibbs Smith, Publisher
P.O. Box 667
Layton, Utah 84041

Orders: (1-800) 748-5439
www.gibbs-smith.com

Designed and produced by Leesha Jones
Printed and bound in Hong Kong

Library of Congress Cataloging-in-Publication Data
Thiede, Cindy Teipner, 1958–
Inside log homes : the art and spirit of home décor / Cindy Thiede; photography by Jonathan Stoke
and Cindy Thiede.—1st ed.
p. cm.
ISBN 10: 0-87905-963-X (hb); ISBN 10: 1-58685-354-6 (pbk) ISBN 13: 978-1-58685-354-9 (pbk)
1. Log cabins—Design and construction. 2. Interior decoration. 3. Architecture, Domestic. I. Title.

TH4840.T47 2000
747—dc21
                    00-030126

With love and gratitude to Martie and Dr. Bill,
my mom and dad.

CONTENTS

Acknowledgements

This is my fifth book on log homes and my fifth foray into the homes and lives of log-home aficionados. While each book is an exposé of distinct and wonderful log homes, for me they also chronicle memorable events and delightful people. How can I forget the simple pleasures of eating catfish and clog dancing in Tennessee, or the time we barely escaped with our lives after a deluge of massive boulders and mud buried a South Carolina highway just seconds ahead of our speeding van? I know I'll never forget that heart-stopping moment when, during a photo shoot in Wyoming, a fireplace damper slammed shut in the midst of a roaring blaze, sending clouds of sooty smoke into the living room of a brand-new million-dollar log home, or my first encounter with Zelda, a hilarious, ripsnortin' bulldog (and master of disguise) who makes a brief appearance in this book.

In these moments and zillions of others, there were people deserving of thanks and recognition. Some of these people are professional acquaintances. Many are homeowners. Some are new friends, and others have been a part of my life for a long time.

Regardless, it is the collective energies and support of many individuals who bring life to each new project and make the "doing" part a joyful event.

In writing and photographing *Inside Log Homes,* I owe a debt of gratitude to the following people and then some:

Thank you, Jonathan Stoke, a worthy, good-natured photographer who has been down this road with me before—never mind impossibly long hours, run-amuck moose, and one too many cans of chicken noodle soup.

Praises to all the named and unnamed homeowners featured in these pages who permitted the pictures and, thus, the book to happen, with special thanks to Carol Gardner and zesty Zelda for latte boosts, inspiration, directions and, most of all, laughter.

More thanks to the many log-home companies, contractors, architects, designers, artisans, and building professionals who were there to assist and answer my questions at every turn—with a very special acknowledgment to Char Thompson, a talented designer and new friend who consulted and encouraged me along the way. Thanks also to Sandra

Willingham, owner of The Gardener, for beautiful bulbs and flowers.

Extra, extra "bigacious" thanks to another new friend, Joella DeVillier, who came to work with me in the last few months of this project. Without a doubt, I never would have stayed on track or had nearly as much fun without her! Multitalented, she's a thorough editor, beautiful poet, creative writer, wistful dreamer, and the fastest net-surfer I've ever met. Not only that, but she knows a good word when she sees one!

Finally, hugs and kisses to my husband and sons—Art, Tyler, and Jesse—and to a few of my best old friends who offered aid at every turn: Heather Pedersen (*never* to be replaced), Lise Mousel-Martini (my best childhood friend who will one day write a real best-seller—maybe about us!), Cary Jones (a dear friend who would grow daisies in Siberia if I asked), Byrd Golay (who thinks outside of the box and makes me laugh out loud), Patrice Cole (my Martha Stewart stand-in), and, last, but not least, our dog Rosie, and Blackberry the cat.

Introduction

We take a tree, or many trees, as our own,

respecting the stories they contain and the lives they have led.

Of them we create a dwelling, made beautiful by their presence and strength

and we live within their warm embrace in a place called home.

—Joella DeVillier

There is a log-cabin ethic at work in America. It is not all about curling wisps of smoke and one-room cabins—although, perhaps, some shared, uncomplicated memory cradles our collective soul. Conscious or not, it has inspired a renewed interest in log homes, one that started back in the 1970s when America propped open one dubious eye for a renewed peek at the ubiquitous log cabin. A few hardy souls grabbed their axes and headed for the woods.

In the 1980s, bona fide builders got into the act. Cabins suddenly got better *and* bigger. By now, both eyes were open wide, and America liked what it saw. Exploratory and a little trendy, the concept of a modern-day log house began to catch on.

The late 1980s and 1990s witnessed architects and interior decorators taking log-cabin design to places our founding fathers could scarcely have imagined. *Cabins* became *homes* or even *castles*, sought out by do-it-yourselfers and boardroom barons alike. Creative minds broke all the rules. Warm and robust, logs were mingled with everything from steel to marble. Huge expanses of glass became expected components of good design. Interiors often cast off traditional attire for fun or in favor of more ethnic, chic, regal, or hip new looks. Decidedly, logs had found their place on the pantry shelves of prominent builders and designers who used them liberally along with the other staples of their trade.

Today, crossing over the threshold into a new millennium, America is comfortable with and confident in log-home living. Surely we know what logs are capable of. All the same, log-home architecture and interior design has never adhered to a "one size fits all" prescript. Nor, despite their versatility, does everything under the sun fit equally well in log homes.

No matter how far-flung the application, the log remains a direct link to things that are earthy and natural. We see it. We feel it in the very marrow of our bones. Logs choose us as much as we choose them. And because logs are what they are—dynamic, vigorous, natural—there is much to learn from them and about them when planning and decorating our homes.

Inside Log Homes is a visual study of the quirky challenges and exciting opportunities we encounter on that journey to "home sweet log home." This journey, however, is mostly about the places inside our homes—where we take our heart-longings and shape our own cabin ethic through the wood, our living space, and our décor. As with any abode, there are zillions of planning and decorating choices. Some, however, are curiously unique to logs.

Starting big, we delve into architecture and the log bones. Size, shape, color, texture, and the rhythms peculiar to shifting, breathing log walls distinguish this design path from one trod upon en route to a frame-built house. Beyond the nuances of walls and the various logistics of space and lighting is the tree's innate flair for artistic expression. Working in harmony with their materials, builders and artisans give articulate rein to timbers, roots, and branches inside a home. Whether structural or purely aesthetic, sculpted openings, prominent trusses, decorative carvings, and rustic twig work are among those special attributes that endear us to this unique building medium.

Strolling past logistics, we turn to the pleasant challenge of interior décor, including favorite options for flooring, countertops, fabrics, and furnishings. Though hardly confined to specifics or bound by rules, logs embrace color and rich texture. Interiors that satisfy our personal desires for comfort, style, pleasure, and whimsy tend to be tactile and warm. Even the most upscale and elegant log-home interiors will invite comfortable use.

Inside Log Homes peeks through doors into hundreds of uniquely styled and personally appointed spaces. Sometimes comfortably familiar, other times surprising and unexpected, each room may plant the seed of possibility or opportunity for your own emerging vision of home and hearth. Even if you'll never own a log home, the insights of homeowners and professional decorators can help you interject a like-minded spirit into your personal space.

From the biggest notions of carefully styled rooms to the smallest comforts and delights of accessorizing a home or garden with your favorite things, *Inside Log Homes* offers suggestions, understanding, and inspiration regarding the intensely personal and expressive world of log-cabin living and décor.

A midwinter day, firelight, and a snug arrangement of comfortable furnishings are the hallmark of this quintessential log home inspired by its owners and interior designer Elizabeth Lucini.

Messing WITH THE BONES

Structural log joists that crisscross the ceiling in many homes support decking that is both the ceiling downstairs and the subfloor upstairs. Unless an expensive secondary floor is laid above that subfloor, there will not be space to hide plumbing pipes, heating ducts, or other home innards that typically ramble from room to room in the gap beneath a floor.

BEGINNINGS

Log-home building is a process. Maybe it starts on a whim—perhaps it's the wistful memory of a pinecone-strewn deck and a tiny lakeside cabin. Maybe it's garden-grown potatoes with your grandma's home-churned butter and your grandpa's dancing dog (the one that smoked a pipe while pirouetting over the wooden floors and hooked rugs in that old log-cabin kitchen). Ah, heck. It might be nothing like that at all. Perhaps you just saw a log house featured in the pages of *Architectural Digest,* and you had no idea logs could be so stylish or so clean! No matter what it is that triggers your personal mission to live in logs, you will have to start with a handful of ideas, the library, and the yellow pages (or, more likely, the yellowpages.com!).

Even if you've collected ideas and clippings for half a lifetime, when you get right down to it, you will probably want to enlist some sort of expert advice from the people who design and decorate log homes. Not because your choices and options are limited, but because—as Carol Fink, co-owner of Alpine Log Homes, asserts—there are more "drop-dead cool" choices and opportunities now than ever before, and you'll want to know where and how to apply them. Well, that, and the fact that logs do march to a slightly different beat.

You have heard it said that logs are alive. This is more than a passing reference to the tangible way whole logs resemble living trees. Logs actually shift and settle in response to their environment. How much so depends on the moisture content of the wood or the weight and structure of the walls that contain them. Not to worry—experienced builders understand this and accommodate these antics in their designs (another good reason to make sure your architect and builder are "logified"). But there is also the matter of log walls. They're solid. The outside wall *is* the inside wall, so logs must be predrilled or otherwise adapted to accommodate electrical wiring or anything else that legions of homebuilders and subcontractors have historically concealed between the studs of conventionally framed walls and floors. Plumbing, heating, air-conditioning, and sound systems may all need tweaking, which, in turn, impacts the way a room shapes up.

Raised platforms under second-floor tubs and toilets can provide flexibility for routing pipes from one side of a room to another. Interior framed walls that carry through to the floor below can conceal vertical runs of pipe or wire. If those aren't an option, built-in chases will also do the trick. (In cold climates, build plumbing chases along interior walls to avoid frozen pipes.)

A good beginning makes a good ending.
—English Proverb

The logs themselves also put very different demands upon the spaces they define. Large logs may dictate bigger rooms, higher ceilings, or larger-scaled furnishings. Also, the shape, color, and texture of the wood contribute powerfully to the character and style of a home. Fourteen-inch-diameter, skip-peeled logs accentuated by stripes of light-colored chink may inspire very different interiors than finely sanded walls of eight-inch whitewashed logs. Beyond that, cabinetry or framed interior walls and partitions must be carefully scribed into the logs for a clean, tight fit. Furniture won't sit flat against round logs, and pictures can tip dizzily on a wall. The list goes on.

This is not to say there isn't cross-over galore between log- and stick-built homes. But, like Darwin's finches, the creatures' dissimilarities warrant special attention. If you know what those differences are and affirm them in your plans, you are more likely to avoid headaches and, worse, costly mistakes later.

The truth is, interior design begins the moment you start penning out floor plans and elevations. You don't shape a room without envisioning the major pieces of furniture that will live in that space or, more importantly, how you and your family will live in that space. Your decorating decisions can often involve spatial and structural concerns that need to be identified early on. A good architect will want to spend some time getting to know you. So will an interior decorator or designer. In fact, jokes one decorator friend, you can get to know each other quite well. You see your clients first thing in the morning— sometimes in their underwear if you're not careful! You share cocktails when the sun goes down and occasionally work into the night. You may even travel to-gether to visit a big-city design center or to hunt down a key piece of furniture. If you intend on hiring a decorator or designer, do it sooner than later. Today's log-home projects are often team efforts

FACING PAGE: Framed walls and built-in furniture require extra attention when they intersect with bumpy logs. Wall coverings or trim boards may have to be pieced in as well. In this bathroom, bark stripped from a birch tree and real twigs paper the wall.

Logs have stature, powerful presence, and sometimes a mind of their own. As the size, scale, and complexity of a home increases, so will the need for log-home know-how. Sometimes, a whole team of veteran design-ers, builders, and artisans will join forces with a homeowner to complete a project. Such was the case with this large home, designed and built by architect Janet Jarvis, Pioneer Log Homes, Mutchler Construction, Beth Cowman Interiors, and a host of other craftsmen and consultants.

DECORATOR OR DESIGNER . . . WHICH IS WHICH?

Decorator or interior designer? Whom do you call when you need help designing and furnishing your home? Is there really a difference? Technically speaking, there is. The title of interior designer implies a certain amount of education not only with fabrics and furnishings but also with various aspects of house planning, drafting, and construction.

Decorators have received no formal architectural education and may be less familiar with some of the technical or internal workings of a house. Experience, however, cannot be discounted, and some of the most acclaimed professionals in the business do not bear a formal title.

Either professional will likely have a keen eye and access to a huge array of resources. If you're starting from scratch or doing a major remodel, use a qualified professional to help you pick first things first and keep you on schedule as you move through the process of simultaneously building and decorating a home.

Either professional may be available for the duration of a building project from the ground up. If that doesn't fit your budget, a month, a week, or sometimes even a day of sound advice can get you over a hump and provide you with enough oomph and direction to embellish the plot and perfect the character of your log-home dream. Before hiring, ask about an individual's experience with log homes, view a portfolio, then ask for and check out references. In the end, no matter how good you perceive experts to be, make sure you really like them and get a sense that they have your personal home and comfort in mind.

with lightbulbs going on when different talents walk through the rooms of your house plan.

When embarking on a log-house project, it is not uncommon to pick a log-building company first and proceed from there. Apart from having competent craftsmen and good working relationships with a variety of general contractors around the country, many log companies have in-house architects and designers who can help you develop and formalize your house plans. These services may even be free if the company moves forward with the

Interior design evolves around the entire house and often begins with a careful evaluation of a home's most permanent features. Whether starting from scratch or redecorating an existing structure, you'll find that exposure, the availability of natural light, the views, window placement, ceiling height, and spatial relationships are important factors to consider.

log work. Furthermore, reputable log companies can help direct you to qualified subcontractors or even lending institutions comfortable with log-home financing.

The other option, of course, is to select your own architect or house designer and/or independent builder. Let experience and reputation help guide your selection, but if you choose an architect without log-home experience, a qualified log builder or log-building company should also be involved early in the process. As with any professional consultant, always discuss fees and your budget up front. Visit www.loghomelists.com for a wealth of information and a state-by-state source of builders and dealers along with listings of log-savvy architects and interior designers. This site also includes a search engine dedicated to the log-home industry.

Large hewn logs and timber-framed trusses form an expansive framework for these open, sun-washed spaces decorated by the owners and their designer, Patricia Schlapp. Furnishings are keyed to and arranged around the immense river-rock fireplace, floor-to-peak windows, and timbered posts. When a new family moved into this home, the walls overhead were bright white. A fresh coat of olive paint brought down the scale of the room and softened angular spaces. A proportionately huge 5-by-7-foot watercolor by New York artist George Harkins combines elements of color, size, and subject to integrate each living space with the streamside landscape outdoors.

"We shape our buildings: thereafter they shape us."—Winston Churchill

Green cedar logs, felled in the spring and peeled by hand, are carefully hand-scribed and saddle-notched for a superb fit. The logs were artfully sanded, with special attention given to the bumps and knobs. Staining and selective bleaching help achieve a uniform color throughout, while a final coat of varnish highlights the grain and gives a rich, warm luster to the wood. The time and labor associated with handcrafted homes typically make them more expensive than homes built with machine-milled logs.

YOU'VE GOT A BONE TO PICK

*T*hink "log house" and what do you see? Dark brown logs with some kind of cotton-colored chinking in between? Maybe your logs are hewn flat and weathered gray or honey colored with no chinking at all. Or maybe your log-home vision is just a vague, cozy, brownish thing that elicits more of an emotional response in your mind's eye than it does a physical portrait with distinct form and color.

When you set out to build a new home, the bones come first, with the possible combinations of log and corner styles being more extensive than you might imagine. Some builders use whole round logs, usually peeling them—but not always. Other craftsmen hew their timbers flat on two, three, or even four sides. And while one corner system might be used more often with square logs than with round ones, most are interchangeable. To make things more interesting, many companies use machines to shape, cope, and notch their logs. These machines are capable of creating some very inventive, though wholly nontraditional, log profiles. There is also the matter of chink—the fill between the horizontal surfaces of the logs. Some buildings are intended to be tight and fitted, while others are meant to have stripes of chink applied lengthwise down the logs. Add stains, whitewashing, or other wood

finishes to the mix and you have a literal smorgasbord of log-home flavors to choose from.

In any given log home, the distinctive shape, color, and texture of the wood can evoke a whole range of mood or emotion. The logs can be quite subtle, just nudging the subconscious into quiet, comfortable realization that they are there at all. Other times, the logs take center stage, eliciting powerful and gutsy responses that, quite literally, stop you in your tracks.

ABOVE: Pattern and texture go wild in a skip-peeled house where the outer bark is removed but fits and spurts of cambium are left intact. Three-sided D-shaped logs with tidy square corners present a simple alternative to other complex and time-consuming forms of log joinery.

LEFT: Hearthstone Homes specializes in squared and hewn log homes that call to mind traditional Appalachian dovetail-style cabins. In this case the logs were rough-sawn then hand-notched. A machine was employed to hew and texture the sides of each log, and the wood was sandblasted. A gray stain visually aged the logs, and same-color chink makes a soft and subtle transition from one log to another.

ABOVE: Three-sided sawn logs make for smooth, flat walls inside. Coated with a nearly transparent finish, these logs have a fresh, bright look. Despite the natural beauty of just-cut wood, interior logs should be sealed to prevent cleaning and maintenance problems later.

FACING PAGE: Homes built with full-round chinked logs are most commonly identified with the western tradition of log building. The presence of strong horizontal lines and tall walls, as in this home designed by architect Larry Berlin and decorated by Liza Bryan, cannot be discounted when choosing fabrics and furnishings for a room.

FINISH YOUR WOOD

Log-home interior finishes come in a variety of different formulas designed to color the wood, highlight the grain, and protect the wood from scrapes and bumps, errant fingerprints, and the absorption of household odors. They also make cleaning and dusting less of a chore.

Interior finishes are of two basic types: stains and sealers. Paint is also used on occasion, but only on extremely well-seasoned logs since it forms a weaker bond with the wood and hard-coats the surface. Any moisture trapped inside the log will actually lift the paint off as it tries to make its way out. Furthermore, the opaque nature of paint masks the very essence of the wood. People don't typically choose logs then completely cover them up, except under special circumstances.

Stains contain color that tints the surface of the log along with other ingredients that penetrate several cell-layers deep into the wood. Stains aren't intended to dry to a hard finish and may feel slightly tacky to the touch. If the logs are left unsealed, dust can glom on. Conversely, sealers are usually clear, stay on top of the wood, and dry to a hard protective finish.

Stains and sealers have historically been oil-based products, but government regulations and new technologies have led to the emergence of a whole new breed of less-toxic water-based finishes. These formulations are nonflammable, less yellowing, and generally more breathable than their predecessors. They sometimes contain UV protectants and may be ideal for light, natural-colored wood. Issues of durability, however, are still subject to strong debate among professionals, so ask your builders which products they use and why.

• Like paint, stains and sealers are defined as having matte, satin, gloss, or semigloss qualities. Consider that a glossy sealer applied over a glossy stain will double the shine.

• Before applying any finish to your walls, do a test sample—the bigger the better. Pick an inconspicuous area on your wall, or use scrap logs from the actual walls to be stained. If in doubt, start with light colors since it's always easier to darken the wood than to lighten it after the fact. Different woods take stain differently—so will the same wood if cut or prepped in a different way. In fact, the color can even vary within a log, so it is important to stay consistent in your application. Brushing is recommended, so don't wipe on a sample and brush on the real thing later. Replicate the same procedures each step of the way. It is common to apply up to three separate coats of finish to an interior wall.

• Plan on sealing your interior log walls even if you want them to appear freshly cut and natural. The logs should be cleaned thoroughly or even power-washed. Power-washing can cause some fuzzing of the wood, and sanding afterward may be necessary for a velvety-smooth finish. At least two coats of a good clear finish are recommended.

• Rustic, partially peeled log houses also need attention inside. Without sealant, the bark will continue to flake off and the wood will gray as surface cells die. A clear matte finish may be a good option to keep the wood looking as natural as possible.

• When applied properly with two to three coats of coverage, interior wall finishes may never need redoing. The exception might be in the immediate area around glass windows and doors that are exposed to high and constant levels of UV radiation. You will also want to touch up any area of the wall that has been scraped or damaged through use.

More than 150 years of weather and age have left these logs distinguished and gray. Wanting the restoration to appear as historically accurate as possible, artisans sometimes use mortar between the logs instead of the more-flexible synthetic chinking materials available today. Cement or mortar chink won't flex with log movement, so it only works with extremely stable wood.

BELOW LEFT: Back when hurried settlers were still hacking their cabins out of the woods, the chink between their logs was an eclectic mix of most anything a family could find to stuff in the cracks. More-refined homes used mortar. In other regions, particularly in the West, sapling poles like these were carefully shaped to fit between the logs. In some areas (for instance, Jackson, Wyoming), the tradition still prevails, though it is both time-consuming and labor-intensive.

The unconventional marriage of corrugated metal, new wood, bright whites, and neutrals is peaceful and soothing despite the remarkable interplay of line and texture. Incandescent lighting is concealed in crown molding that starts above the window and runs around the perimeter of the room.

LOGS—A LITTLE OR A LOT?

*A*s you step into the arena of home possibilities, you may also ask, "How much log is enough?" Today's homes are rarely log from top to bottom and side to side. Logs are imminently mix-and-matchable with a variety of other materials such as glass, stucco, stone, or even more industrial materials like copper and steel. Some combinations are rooted in regional and cultural traditions like the log and stucco hybrids that have evolved out of the vast, fluid landscape of the American Southwest. Others are easy marriages with other natural materials. Still others are contemporary offshoots based on the notion that opposites really do attract. In the interest of cost or to ease the technical challenges inherent in building log-roof systems, gable ends may be framed or merely sided with logs. Framing also permits the introduction of other building materials such as shingles and shakes, stucco, or board-and-batten siding.

Sometimes, an all-log house can feel oppressive or dark. While exterior walls may be wood through and through, at least some of the interior walls can be framed to provide a break from the logs and make way for wall art, decorative paper, and paint (not to mention hiding places for pipes and wiring). Likewise, post-and-beam construction, timber-frame construction, and the increasingly popular notion of using logs for "accent" have also crept into the repertoire of possibility. Each of these options affords different freedoms in terms of design, and satisfies homeowners' varying tastes and sensibilities.

Framed walls generally take up less space inside a home as well. In fact, if you aren't careful, big logs will gobble up floor space when you aren't looking. On paper, a pen-and-ink outline won't reflect the space taken up by a twelve-inch log.

Nor is it uncommon for log companies and home designers to base room size on measurements taken from the center of one wall to the center of another. Several inches here and there may not seem significant until you take into account the accumulative bite of all four walls. The impact can be particularly unsettling in smaller rooms and closets.

And while you're thinking about your logs, remember that intersecting log walls can result in big, beefy corner sections. We tend to think about these corners as being visible only on the outside of a home, but that isn't always the case. When corners happen to turn inward, their presence will be felt inside a room. In other configurations, one log wall will join with another in the middle. While there won't be an intrusive corner to plan around, there will be a vertical stack of log ends poking into your space and creating a little jog in the wall that could thwart certain furniture arrangements. Homeowners don't disdain these trespasses. After all, they love their logs. They are, however, something to anticipate and plan around.

Pliable and free-flowing, a framework of stucco and plaster softens and complements log walls.

Log ends can project into a room at any point on a wall, depending on the layout and construction of a house. They can be trimmed back some if necessary, but planning ahead will help you accommodate individual pieces of furnishings that want to back up against a wall.

BELOW: Wrapped in the cool soft greens of summertime, this transparent living room has no log walls—only massive pine posts and nearly floor-to-ceiling panels of transparent glass. Post-and-beam construction works well with so much glass since vertical posts form a stable framework. On the other hand, horizontal stacks of logs can settle over time, and may need to be specially designed or reinforced with steel rods to keep large expanses of glass from cracking.

When Betsy and Michael Rudigoz decided to remodel their small log house, they chose to add on with a combination of timber frame and Sheetrock. The combination was less expensive than full-log construction and appeased their appetite for "European country." Some of the timbers were recycled from the home's original log garage while others were salvaged from a restaurant demolition in a neighboring ski town. Betsy re-sanded all the logs and timbers then stained the salvaged wood and her existing yellow pine walls with a much darker mixture concocted through trial and error.

"Individual trees can seize the imagination and win your heart."
—*Thomas Moore*

A hammer-beam truss cast in hewn timbers stands in moving contrast to round log walls. The gently arched passageway below mirrors the curve of the truss and creates another level of interest while bringing the scale of the large space into human perspective. Hung simply on rail spikes pounded into the logs, a wagon wheel completes the picture.

LET THE TREES SPEAK!

From its poetic tangle of roots to the shapely contours of its supple branches, the tree has long been an inspired source of art and beauty. Inside the home, whole trunks embody the essence, strength, and mystery of the forest. As a raw product of nature, the log is as the sculptor's clay—there to be carved and transformed into images of grace or fancy. Curvaceous branches lend themselves to spontaneous weavings and decorative rails. Burled wood, formed naturally as the tree defends itself from parasitic attack, is humorous, touchable, and intriguing.

PREVIOUS PAGE: Lying on his back atop scaffolding, Oregon artisan Paul Stark used a chain saw and chisels to carve the head, body, and twenty-foot wingspan of this stylized eagle.

RIGHT: Homeowner Suzi McKinney designed this family room addition to her family's log-and-stucco home in Idaho. A short afternoon of log-yard scrounging turned up the bentwood pieces that builder Art Thiede puzzled together into this pleasing rustic arch. The extra effort and installation of the passage adds much to the design but cost little more than some other plain-Jane approach. Sculpted stucco panels infill space previously taken up by large picture windows.

Root-based posts have become a sort of trademark in houses built by Oregon Log Homes. First used by the owners in their own company showplace, the interpretive posts can be utilized almost anywhere, from railings to door frames.

Used in a big way, the logs give shape and substance to a room. Massive trusses and sculpted passageways help set the emotional pace. Indeed, we are awed by them, sometimes even called to build with logs because of them. Arches, curved posts, and roaming twigs can become the focal point of a room or serve to soften the powerful interplay of vertical and horizontal lines inherent in log walls.

Some of these artistic and structural displays are expensive, requiring extensive skill, planning, and labor. Other times, an irregular log in a woodworker's heap will script itself into a design in the midst of building. Large or small, opportunities for individual expression are the gift and reward of giving voice to the stature or inherent natural beauty of the tree.

*Every flowing ring and swirl of grain
paints a pattern of joy or pain.
Perhaps a season of parching drought,
or a time of plenteous nourishment.
A tree leaves a tale that we may read
if we but look.
Each tree—a book.*   —JOELLA DEVILLIER

ABOVE: Limber pine roots and twigs appear to sprout from the base of this stacked-wood fireplace surround and log mantel. Actually, Doug Tedrow custom-fitted them with the homeowner throwing in her two cents as well. Doug likes to involve his clients when he can because they often have a precise notion of how "random" should look. Besides that, they think it's fun!

FACING PAGE: Washington craftsman Gary Espe has an eye for character—and a barn full of coarse, bark-on limbs and dirty stumps hauled from the woods. Transforming them into works of functional art is one of his specialties. This stairway was a labor of love and a splurge for the owners, but it is also one of the best-loved features in their home.

ABOVE: A forked and twisted trunk reaches skyward. Subtle yet provocative, it begs look after look.

RIGHT: Rustic, western, and light-hearted, a breezeway full of burled pine posts sets this house apart in Wilson, Wyoming.

To a wood sculptor, posts and log ends are like a canvas waiting for paint. Oregon artisan J. Chester Armstrong carved this fanciful newel post into a trio of curious otters for clients who adored those fun-loving creatures.

THE LIVABLE SPACE

$\mathcal{W}$e live in spaces—eating spaces, bathing and sleeping spaces, working and playing spaces. Our houses are creative arrangements of those spaces, and successful interiors might be measured best by how well each space functions and by the personal enjoyment it gives us. In that sense, log homes are no different from any other type of house, and good planning and interior design begin with a thorough analysis of the size, shape, architectural attributes, and intended use of each room. On the other hand, logs are logs, so the mechanics and aesthetics of construction may give pause to some new ways of thinking.

Consider first the size of the logs and how they impact a space. Walls stacked with large logs may feel squatty in small rooms with average ceiling heights. Conversely, a twenty-five-foot wall built with small logs can feel vast and disproportionate without visual breaks such as well-proportioned windows, wall hangings, or other interesting architectural elements. Big spaces in general are near and dear to many a homeowner's heart. The great room has become a popular concept in American architecture, and in terms of log construction, a family's first or most memorable encounter may well have been in the celebrated lobby of a national park lodge. As homeowners pay homage to the stature of logs and remake those memories into personal space, there is a tendency toward grand rooms with soaring ceilings. When properly planned and thoughtfully furnished, these spaces will be wonderful and well used. The challenge, however, is to create an inviting environment that can be enjoyed by a family when the party's over and the guests have gone home.

Not only are exceedingly large spaces expensive to build, they can also be difficult to heat, cool, and maintain. Bulbs burn out, and easily managed ladders or cleaning wands only go so high. Beyond that, the grand scale of huge rooms frequently calls for larger furnishings. This makes perfect sense, since stout pieces match the stature of log walls, while overstuffed chairs and cushy pillows invite comfort and intimacy. Just don't go too far. Decorators emphasize that things can actually get too big, and in an effort to scale the size of the furniture to the room, you can lose sight of human perspective. When everything is larger than life, we tend to be more lost than comforted.

• Rather than overscaling everything in a large space, create separate furniture arrangements to accommodate smaller groups or different activities such as dining and game playing. Experts

There is no rule that says furniture needs to back up against the walls or line up at right angles. Here a triangular arrangement of sofas and chairs hones the conversation area into a comfortable zone around the fireplace. It also opens up the area behind the couch to accommodate traffic from the kitchen to the dining area. A wonderful niche tucked away at the opposite end of the room offers a gracious, semiprivate retreat.

suggest that a distance of four to ten feet between sofas and chairs is ideal for promoting comfortable conversation.

• Use different-sized and -shaped area rugs to divide a room and anchor individual groupings.

• Tuck nooks and comfortable crannies into a room. Window seats and little alcoves can feel cozy and exceptionally private, even in a large space.

• Regardless of size, each room should have a dramatic element that draws your attention. It might be any number of things, from a large picture window to a prominent fireplace, wonderful staircase, or eye-catching chandelier. In oversized spaces, you will

Lonely moments are whiled away in this special nook that draws both children and adults. Who knows what's stowed beneath the built-in seats? Games, linens, or Christmas decorations, perhaps? The trunk also holds promise for stored items that might help transform this gentle space into a play area or sleeping nook.

"Always design a thing by considering it in its next larger context— a chair in a room, a room in a house, a house in an environment." —Eliel Saarinen

Cotton paisley drapes and beautifully proportioned windows break up this expansive log wall and create a stunning backdrop for the chivalric bronze created by New Mexico artist Star Lianna York. Since this room is relatively long and narrow, there was a lot of dead space left in the corners and around the edges after homeowner Elizabeth Tierney and decorator Terri DeMun had grouped the primary furnishings in front of the fireplace. They used such things as the sculpture in front of the window and a meticulously restored barber's pole and chair in the corner to balance out the space and create additional areas of interest around the room.

FACING PAGE: Timber-frame trusses match the grandeur of the mountain view in this sapling-chinked living room designed for the enjoyment of its year-round residents and the frequent comings and goings of three generations of extended family. Two massive elk-antler chandeliers span more than six feet each, but they feel right because they are in proportion to the size and scale of the room. Similarly, the furnishings had to have weight and mass, but they are arranged in separate groupings that break the space into comfortable areas of use.

frequently have more than one focal point to plan around, such as a fireplace at one end of a room and a breathtaking picture-window view off to the side. You can enlist those elements to create separate areas of use. For instance, one arrangement may entice nighttime leisure around the fireplace while the other will have you sporting binoculars to watch an errant moose rambling through your garden (oh, no—not again!)

•   One or more large, attractive light fixtures that drop down into a room can serve as another visual tier and balance out vast amounts of empty vertical space. In like fashion, a tall unbroken expanse of log wall can be reapportioned by hanging large tapestries, quilts, and rugs, unique architectural ornaments such as Victorian gingerbread, an iron gate, and old window frames, or such ever-popular recreational gear as canoes, sleds, and snowshoes.

Finally, when you honestly analyze your need for space, you might discover that super-sizing your room is not in your family's best interests. After all, if our log home sensibilities aren't rooted in grand lodges, chances are they are fixed to

images found on jugs of maple syrup or childhood tins of Lincoln Logs.

Montana designer Hilary Heminway promotes the concept of cluster living. Rather than make do with one gigantic space, she encourages clients to create additional smaller rooms or better yet, separate outbuildings. Having spent part of each of the past twenty-five years on a Montana ranch, she has cut her teeth on western tradition and bunkhouse culture that accommodates varying numbers of ranch hands from season to season. In terms of family living, smaller buildings are practical and easy to care for. When the relatives are gone, an outbuilding can be turned off and locked up. Undoing some of the usual mind-sets, Hilary also finds that restored sheepherders' wagons and canvas tepees make wonderful, whimsical living spaces in due season.

A REASON FOR ROOM

A fisherman's niche for tying flies, an indoor spigot above the dog's water bowl in the mudroom, a cellar for wine: when laying out a home, it is sometimes the little spaces and thoughtful extras that make a good house great! Think about the way your family lives, then tailor your home to accommodate your habits and hobbies. That's not necessarily to say "build bigger." Instead, you can enlarge your home's practical value by planning and furnishing rooms for multiple uses. A convertible couch in the office or an armoire with a fold-down desk in the guest room are obvious ways to overlap space and function. But what about installing a drain in the mudroom floor so you can wash down the dogs? Or, add seasons of use to enclosed porches by trading screens out for Plexiglas in the

This catwalk serves as a transition from the master suite on one side of the house to guest bedrooms on the other side while capturing extra living space in between. It also over-looks both the living area and entry down below. Catwalks are popular in log homes with large spaces and engaging trusses since they put you at eye level with the logs. When viewed from below, they also serve to bring down the scale of soaring spaces.

fall and factoring in a heat source. Include small tables or bed trays for dining in a guest room or for morning coffee in the master bath. TV tables are big fun in the family room for pizza and movie night with the kids. Kitchens and dining rooms are frequent stand-ins for a small home office, student's study hall, or arts and crafts space. Make them more convenient by dedicating space in cabinets, drawers, or shelves for books and supplies.

Truth be known, you can never have too much dedicated storage—not just one big closet tucked under the stairs, but cabinets and drawers and little surprise storage spaces tucked away in every room. Since a good bit of carving and cajoling goes along with the installation of built-in cabinetry against log walls, freestanding pieces of furniture are most welcome.

This detailed wildlife sculpture is a favorite of owners Jim and Barbara Ryan. Designer Char Thompson made it a focal point in the home and used it to check the uninterrupted flow of space from the living room at one end of the house to the kitchen at the other. The sculpture, highlighted by special lights in the ceiling, is also a fountain. The plumbing works are concealed within its finely crafted base. Preplanning was essential, and the piece was included in the architectural drawings of the house. In lieu of an area rug, a lush square of carpet is inset into radiant-heat floors.

The owner of this upscale trapper's cabin near Aspen, Colorado, went to great lengths to hide the evidence of modern technology, including the kitchen. The stovetop, microwave oven, sink, dishwasher, and mini-fridge (complete with icemaker) are completely concealed behind the hand-rubbed doors of this freestanding, custom-crafted armoire.

BELOW: Full guest bathrooms with every bedroom are expensive to install and often unnecessary. At this family retreat, sinks installed in conjunction with bedroom closets were a happy compromise. A compact staircase made of wood blocks spirals up to a tiny loft for the kids. Though artfully done and efficient in its use of space, such a staircase may not be allowed under some local building codes.

SUN-KISSED: WINDOWS TO YOUR WORLD

No matter how charming the picture of Grandma's cabin in the woods, her itty-bitty windows are mostly a thing of the past. Today, lots of light-conscious glass is often high on the must-have list. Of course, many log homes are located in rural areas where blue sky or mountain scenery abounds, and the beauty of a space can rest, in part, on the view. The placement, size, and orientation of windows will affect the function, aesthetics, and arrangement of a space. The shape and style of a window can feature prominently into room design. Knowing where and when the sun rises and sets in a room may dictate how you use and organize your space. East-facing windows bring in morning light. South-facing windows drink in hours of midday sun, and west-facing windows get that intense burst of late-afternoon sun. Meanwhile, north-facing windows don't bring in much natural light at all.

Owners Bruce and Gretchen Willison borrowed the concept for leaded, diamond-paned windows from an Adirondack lodge in upstate New York. Used only in the upper portion of the windows, the custom-made panes add texture and discriminating detail without obstructing the view. This east-facing room gets welcome morning sun, so the draperies are rarely drawn.

Open ceilings were not an option in this small family home since intricate truss work wasn't in the budget and second-floor space was needed for the bedrooms. Tucked away in private, shady woods, this house does not get an overabundance of sun. Instead of window coverings, the builder chose a framework of contrasting trim and decorative corner blocks. Trimming out a window can pose some interesting dilemmas, particularly on round logs. While this trim is placed on top of the logs, it is also common to back-cut the wood so the trim sits flush against the log.

If west-facing windows leave you running for shade just as you're sitting down with a cup of tea to watch the evening news, window coverings will also be on your list. In fact, window coverings or sun protection should be on your mind long before that. Since log-home owners often pay dearly for their views, there is a tendency to shy away from any shades and draperies unless privacy is an issue. Families will plan for coverings in their bedrooms but refuse them in other view-conscious rooms. Depending on where you live and the exposure of your house, this can be a huge mistake. High-altitude mountain cabins are particularly susceptible to damaging UV rays. Even when the sun's rays aren't coming in directly, reflective light bouncing off a winter snowscape can harm wood and furnishings.

Café curtains offer a sort of happy medium between the love of light and issues of privacy or sun protection. Since most visitors tend to be elk or deer, these curtains are usually open. Papering on the framed wall tells a western story, and the baker's rack is ideal for linens and family photos. Notice how this window and trim are completely contained within the log walls.

If you've ever doubted the sun's potential to fade and discolor, try this simple experiment. Place sheets of colored construction paper in different spots around a home. Affix smaller opaque cutouts to each piece then leave them undisturbed for two to three weeks. Finally, peek under the cutouts. Compare them with fresh sheets of paper and to each other. Obviously, the paper won't be as colorfast as your floors and furnishings, but you will get a relative idea of the sun's intensity in a given area of your home.

There are plenty of options when it comes to controlling the sunshine that we love so much—to be warm in winter and cool in summer, and to see the views we pay for. The time to discuss those options, however, is during the initial design phase of a home. Firstly, aesthetics and structural concerns in log homes may dictate increases in the space between window openings and adjacent walls or other windows. When large sections of wood are removed from a log wall to make way for windows, that wall is weakened. Depending on how much wood is removed, additional engineering or structural reinforcement may be necessary. Beyond that, large windows may call for expansive drapery or other decorative treatments. Architects need to design "stacking" space alongside windows to prevent open curtains from overlapping the glass. Shutters, too, need lots of room around the edges when they're open. Motorized screens and shades are growing increasingly popular in homes with sky-high fenestration or clerestory windows located two and three stories up on a wall. Wiring, however, must be run up to the motors, and while some systems are triggered by battery-operated remotes, others entail the installation of switch plates on the walls and more drilling or finagling around the logs.

Start with the Glass

Companies manufacture a variety of different glass types designed to help warm or cool a home. Tints, multiple layers of glazing, gas-filled space between windowpanes, and special low-E coatings are some of the many ways to improve energy efficiency, reduce UV radiation, and buffer noise. Durable, scratch-resistant adhesive-backed films can also be retrofitted to problem windows but are not typically used in cold climates.

The technology is constantly improving, and companies are making bold claims about their ability to block out the voracious UV radiation that preys on wood and furnishings. Window specialists may tell you that some manufacturers are better than others, and in their experience, not all windows make good on their claims. Just check before you buy; speak with area homeowners who have lived with various products for at least a year. Be aware that tinted windows and retrofitted films are darkened slightly and will cut down on light around the clock. For more information, visit the Efficient Windows web site at www.efficientwindows.org.

Stained, frosted, or other types of decorative glass can feature prominently in design and provide attractive alternatives to window coverings. However, they may not be energy-efficient and, depending on the building codes in a given area, may need to be installed along with additional insulated panes.

In the end, a careful evaluation of your space often results in a little mixing and matching of glass types to maximize comfort and efficiency in each room of your home.

Sunscreen Shades

Sunscreen shades are widely used, particularly at high altitudes. Made of very flat synthetic material, these screens are washable and exceptionally durable. When lowered, you can still see through them, yet they will protect floors and furniture and keep a room from over-heating in the midst of the afternoon. If desired, a second treatment can be used to further dress the window, create a focal point in the room, or underscore the room's décor.

Motorization

Motorization can be adapted to almost any window dressing inside a home. It is also used for retractable awnings installed over windows on exterior walls. Though there will be some added expense, it can be extremely practical for windows where alternatives call for excessively long cords, wands, or nothing at all. The mechanization is not obtrusive and can easily be hidden from view through careful installation or simple secondary window treatments such as valances. If you use a remote, be sure to give it a designated home where it won't get lost. Like curious puppies, they have a way of disappearing at the most inopportune times!

Insulated Coverings

Homes built with large expanses of glass, located in extreme climates, or occupied only part of each year are good candidates for heavier, insulated window coverings. Tight-fitting, insulating shades and lined draperies act like blankets to prevent heat loss or gain at different times of the year. When you're away, they help moderate the temperature inside while keeping your furnishings and collectibles a mystery to curious onlookers. Heavy draperies also absorb sound

Stained and frosted glass wraps this bathing area in shimmering color and light. Mirrors behind the tub and over the vanity make this small room feel as if it goes on forever. There is no call for additional window coverings with the exception of the lace curtain in the door leading to the master bedroom.

An open balcony is a malleable multiple-use space. A restful niche by design, it can be counted on in a pinch for such things as accommodating overnight drop-ins or babysitting school-age kids. The wide-open space draws your attention upward—in this case, to an impressive two-story bay with walls of light-drenching windows. Discreet and hardly noticeable, motorized shades are lowered when necessary by pushing buttons on a hand-held remote.

and can help improve the acoustics in high-ceilinged spaces or rooms with stone floors and other hard surfaces.

Porch Overhangs and Landscaping

Window coverings are not the only way to help regulate the sun. Roof overhangs, awnings, and covered porches will protect your exterior log walls and shade the inside of a room. Landscaping with a mixture of deciduous and evergreen trees and shrubs can also be used creatively around a home. Summertime shade from a large deciduous tree can block out a substantial amount of harmful UV and cool down interiors by several degrees. In the winter, when the leaves are gone, the sun is back in all its warmth and glory. Evergreen trees, on the other hand, protect and shade all year long.

Light from Above

What if your views aren't grand? Suppose you're surrounded by thick shady woods or cozy covered porches. Maybe you don't want to trade wall space for windows, or perhaps you have a central room in the house where windows aren't an option. Any one of these scenarios may give reason to consider skylights. They can be operable or not, and the type of roof along with your climate may make certain types of skylights and methods of installation more practical than others. In cold climates, the certainty and literal weight of heavy snowfall will come under consideration. Snow typically melts on glass placed over heated spaces, but skylights located in porch roofs over exterior decks or in second homes that don't get used in the winter may need periodic clearing.

Slatted blinds with cords and wands can be attractive and economical coverings for windows. They will, however, obscure some portion of the window when open: the longer the window, the wider the stack. In this wood-paneled room, matching blinds blend easily with both the walls and the burled-and-fringed furnishings designed by New West in the style associated with famed Wyoming furniture maker Thomas C. Molesworth.

BELOW: Log posts and beams support a catwalk over the entry of this Wyoming home and frame an impressive view in the great room ahead. The round-top window parrots log and metal trusses inside the house and outside over the deck. The outdoor truss supports a substantial roof overhang that affords relief from an overdose of sun without squelching the view. Notice the line and form of the wall and how stacks of horizontal logs between the windows differ visually from posts.

SHEDDING LIGHT ON LOGS

People are drawn to logs by the warmth of the wood. There is a heart cry for "cozy," the kind we find in a firelit room or glimpse through cabin windows aglow under a starry sky. What we sometimes forget is that, historically, cozy also meant "dark" when it came to log cabins. Today's builders counter that partly with larger, well-placed windows designed to welcome in the daylight. Equally important, artificial light is an entity unto itself, requiring additional planning in log homes.

The fact is, logs do tend to be darker than other plastered, painted, or papered walls. Even light-stained wood absorbs more light than it reflects. Furthermore, the light that is reflected is typically warmer than it would be in other forms of construction. That means it often takes more light to achieve the same level of illumination. Since log-home architecture also glories in high spaces with striking trusses and beam work, there may be call for additional or accent lighting in the ceiling. Finding practical and unobtrusive ways to install fixtures in vaulted ceilings may pose one challenge, while wiring solid log walls generally poses another. Though last-minute additions may be possible in miscellaneous framed walls or by hiding wires behind chinking lines, the time to finalize your interior and exterior lighting plan is before the walls go up—and most certainly before the roof goes on.

In-house lighting systems with centrally located control panels and preselected lighting scenes are increasingly popular in today's log homes. In such a system, switches, knobs, and dimmers (or "wall acne" in lighting

Vaulted ceilings in general pose their own unique problems. Recessed lighting set in close to the roof may not be practical in cold-climate homes since it tends to create hot spots in the roof. Those can lead to snowmelt and the subsequent buildup of ice dams. Track lighting on ceiling beams is one solution and pendant lighting that hangs down from the ceiling is another. In this Wyoming home, recessed cans were avoided altogether. Instead, architect Kristoffer Prestud and interior designer Jacqueline Jenkins opted for a mix that includes an antique crystal chandelier over the dining room table and low-voltage halogen pendant lights over the wet bar in the kitchen. Those compact fixtures put out big light for their size. Blue Murano glass shades soften the relatively harsh light from the bulbs.

"We owe a lot to Thomas Edison—if it wasn't for him, we'd be watching television by candlelight."——Milton Berle

The designers of Bruce and Gretchen Willison's home created a beautifully lit gallery to separate spaces and organize the flow of the house. Exquisite custom lights from Lamps By Hilliard emphasize the architecture of dark-stained columns and establish a well-lit path from the kitchen at one end of the house to the media room at the other end. A matched set of oversized, fallow-deer antler chandeliers from England help create further distinction between the dining area and the living room. Furniture groupings were mapped out very early on, and designer Beth Cowman knew they would need at least five in-floor electrical outlets for wall and table lamps in the living area alone.

lingo) are replaced by a small wall panel with carefully labeled buttons. All the lights in a room or a zone are controlled from this one discreet station. Not only is there a lot less stuff to stick on and in log walls, but those buttons can be pre-programmed to dial up certain moods. For example, one dining room setting may be for "cocktails," another for "supping," and yet another, fully lit, for "cleanup" after the party. These systems add to the cost of a home, but in log homes, labor savings may partially mitigate some of the expense. Regardless, aesthetics, added convenience, and the fun factor may make it all worthwhile.

As you're setting the mood inside your home, don't overlook the importance of exterior and landscape lighting along the way. Without proper illumination outside, those big, beautiful, view-conscious windows by day become black holes by night. They also turn into mirrors. If you want your guests to "use the powder room rather than the large bay window for grooming and teeth cleaning," Glenn Johnson of Spectrum

FACING PAGE: The empty room is a palette for light and color; hammer-beam trusses add shape and dimension to this dramatic space designed by architect Janet Jarvis, and a massive three-tiered chandelier from Naos Forge brings down the vertical scale of the room in a grand way. A pair of sconces flanks the picture window and creates a resting place for the eyes at a comfortable height above the floor. In the foreground, a regal moose is highlighted over the fireplace to provide yet another point of focus in the room.

THINK SCONCE

Mounting wall sconces on big, round, irregular logs may be a little like stuffing square pegs into round holes. If the mounting plate is flat, you may have to scoop out a portion of the wood for a proper fit. If that solves one problem, however, it might create another. When a fixture is set into the wall, shades may start bumping into the logs. One solution is to mount sconces on inconspicuous, specially built boxes attached to the wall. Another is to purchase fixtures that won't be impeded by the logs. Remember, too, that logs are stacked at alternating heights around a room. You can certainly mount a pair of sconces at the same height on a single log, but if you want another pair on an adjacent wall, they will typically have to be placed one log higher or lower to avoid ending up in the chink line.

Lighting needs vary within a room and from space to space. A multilayered plan typically includes a combination of task, accent, decorative, and general ambient light to enhance the nighttime atmosphere. In this bar and entertainment area, there is a little bit of everything. Task lighting under the cabinets is directed at the countertops while accent lights inside the cabinets and above them highlight glassware and objects on display. Decorative carafes of brandy sit on stair-step, glass-lined shelves that are lit from below. The log beam built into the wall on the far left also conceals a strip of lights aimed up at the wall.

Lighting Design in Salt Lake City suggests that you add lights under the eaves or illuminate plantings out in the yard. Exterior path and porch lighting adds an element of safety while other forms of exterior lighting on and around a home can enhance its nighttime beauty. A good exterior lighting plan will also be sensitive to the potential effects of light pollution. In other words, don't overdo it. If turning your cabin into a Christmas tree doesn't vex the neighbors, it may well detract from the beauty and brilliance of a pristine night sky.

This catwalk passes over a foyer and living room below. When a cathedral ceiling made it difficult to bring directed light into the passage, a series of sconces were sculpted into the short walls lining the way.

While most of this home's moody glow emanates from rooms lit from the inside, an exterior lighting plan provides illumination under the eaves and at strategic spots around the deck and rock wall. While not overdone, there is enough light outside to prevent "black wall feeling," a phenomenon that occurs when big picture windows overlook unlit landscapes in the black of night. In typical fashion, the log shell for this custom home was first built off-site, in this case by Canadian-based Unique Log and Timber Works, Inc.

A flat ceiling in Tom and Eliza-beth Tierney's hewn-log home enabled the design of this refined coffered canopy over the upscale living room. Wire-brushed cedar panels are recessed beneath a sea-green copper frame. Dimmers regulate lights concealed inside around the perimeter.

A lamp-lit room has a wonderful ambience that can't be duplicated with overhead lights alone. Translucent lamp shades constructed from materials such as tinted craft paper, mica, and rawhide will mellow the light and give it a much warmer feel than other dense or stark-white materials.

AUDIO SPECIALISTS

Solid, bumpy log walls, soaring ceilings, and dramatic architecture go hand in hand with today's log homes. Such factors, in combination with consumer interest in extensive home sound systems and complex media centers, may dictate extra help from an audio specialist. Audio engineers can configure systems that are accessible from the shower to the backyard. They can work through wiring difficulties, direct speaker placement, or develop a "sweet spot" for best-ever sound when you kick back in your favorite chair. As with lighting professionals, they should be involved early in the planning process.

THE SOUND OF YOUR LIFE

Music, color, poetry—such are the beautiful things in life that bring us joy. Music, like other sensual things, can be therapeutic, dramatic, or entertaining. It is nearly always a part of our lives, and some people go to great lengths to incorporate extravagant sound systems into the fabric of their homes. While the acoustics in log homes can be superb, log architecture also differs from conventional construction in ways that an astute audio buff will want to consider.

The experts say that logs are often "brighter" when it comes to sound. This means that sound waves can bounce around on bumpy walls, making it hard to control their direction. Large furnishings, bookcases at the end of a room, and heavy draperies can help absorb and diffuse these errant waves, as can wall hangings and tapestries. Certain speaker technologies may also work better than others.

Pre-wiring is key, and, as the old cliché states, "the more the merrier." Solid logs present the same problems for audio technicians that they do for the electrician. Wiring is cheap, says Michael Clair of Audio Visual Design Group, but retrofitting is very expensive!

Soaring-ceiling syndrome must also be factored in for quality sound. Although people are tempted to place speakers high overhead and out of sight, acoustics dictate that they stay closer to human height. If they are too high, the sound will be focused in the ceiling area and may be harsh and echoing rather than true and intimate.

Where to put those speakers—now that's a question. While this can be a mild dilemma in any home, it's particularly bothersome for log-home owners who shy from the visual rub of high-tech alongside logs. Speakers are easier to mount and hide among framed and sheetrocked walls if you have them. Speaker grilles can even be faux-painted to blend in with the décor. In lieu of framing, however, speakers must be freestanding, installed in the ceiling, or bolted to the logs. Cabinetry is often employed as a hiding spot, while other times, the largest part of a speaker, or "sub-woofer," can be placed in the floor. We met one inventive homeowner who had his camouflaged behind a large, dark "cat's-eye," or knotty blemish, in a log that faced his kitchen island. A portion of the irregular surface was trimmed away and the sub-woofer hidden behind it. You could walk by it a hundred times and never see it. With the sub-woofer out of the way, the "tweeter," or less-obtrusive little speaker part, can then be mounted on a wall.

While you're incorporating the joys of sound into your life, picture this: surround sound, a bowl of microwave popcorn, and a digitally colored version of *Gone with the Wind* playing on a big screen in your personal home theater. While a lifetime supply of movie tickets for everyone in your neighborhood—or town—might be cheaper, this is an increasingly popular scenario in modern America. Elaborate home-entertainment systems can start at $10,000 and creep up to half a million, so you'll want to ask questions, employ a certified designer, and purchase products with warranties. Key in www.ultimatehometheater.com

for the latest and greatest information on home-theater products and services.

READY—SET—GO! MEASURE AND SKETCH

To help you analyze the spaces in a new or existing home, make a list of the different activities each room will accommodate. Where are the views and when does the sun shine in? Should it be a private space or a gathering spot? How much storage do you need and where will you put that Christmas tree? Before you tackle furniture, take careful measurements of each room. Where are the doors and which way do they swing? When determining how much wall space you have, account for every opening along with stacking space for anticipated window dressings. Note the distance between floors and ceilings and between windowsills and floors. If windows are quite low to the ground, you might position chairs and a small side table there instead of a couch. Don't forget to account for trim work that will eventually frame your doors and windows. That information may or may not be on a floor plan, but it will make a big difference when trying to fit your 5-foot 3-inch hutch into a space that suddenly shrunk eight inches after the door and window trim were installed.

Note where intersecting corners or vertical stacks of log ends project into a room. Centrally located structural posts also tend to be more common in log homes. Whether "well placed" or "in the way" is likely to be in the eye of the beholder. Make a distinction between flat or framed walls in each space and the ones built with bumpy logs. Furniture placement and your choice of art or wall décor may depend on it. Note where outlets, wall switches, heating vents, and overhead light fixtures are or where you want them to be. Dining rooms, for instance, can be particularly fussy if you want to center a fixture over your table but don't yet have the table (or the buffet, or the hutch, or the . . . !).

Traffic flow around furniture and from room to room will also be important. In the dining room, seated adults need around 12 to 16 inches of clearance behind their chairs. The optimal distance between the couch and the TV is three times the size of a screen, or 90 inches for a 30-inch screen. In a typical bedroom, leave 24 inches between the edge of a bed and the wall. Of course, these are merely guidelines. Nothing is cast in stone, and, ultimately, you will make adjustments to accommodate a seven-foot spouse or four rambunctious kids. The real key lies in being aware and planning ahead.

Keep a small notebook with measurements and sketches handy in your car or purse. You never know when you'll stumble onto the ideal piece of artwork or furniture—or at least it will be if it fits!

INTEGRATED HOME AUTOMATION SYSTEMS

More and more of today's log homes are incorporating increasingly popular computer-regulated, low-voltage control systems that give homeowners mastery over their lights, security systems, home theaters, phone systems, appliances, and much more with the touch of a button. While quite expensive, these systems work exceptionally well in log homes since a single control pad can replace dozens of individually wired switches and dimmers. Pre-planning is essential, however, and whole-house automation consultants should be involved before the walls go up. For the most complete directory of home-automation sites, visit www.home-automation.org.

THE *Inside* STORY

The Arts & Crafts movement initiated in England in the latter part of the nineteenth century was, at its core, an artistic reform intent on changing the world. Much like log-home architecture today, it sought solace in a simpler life, the honest pleasure of natural materials, and quality craftsmanship. Though log-walled, Ed and Shirley Cheramy's rec room is recognizably done in the Craftsman style and includes a restored 1905 Brunswick Mission-style pool table, with original furnishings and fixtures by Gustav Stickley and other famed artisans of the day.

"Style is the dress of thoughts."—Philip Dormer Chesterfield

YOUR STORY

When you furnish a home, you fill it with the essence of, well . . . you. Naturally, good interior design is about living day to day. Rooms may be designed to accommodate jelly-coated fingers, muddy boots, a festive party, or a good night's sleep. They will be filled with colors you like and furnishings you use. In essence, they will support you through the practical rigors and pleasures of daily life. Good interiors will do that, but better interiors will nurture your passion for life, not just help you live it. They will reflect something of the things you hold to be true or the things you aspire to. Infuse them with humor, indulge a fantasy, inspirit a dream.

That you choose logs is in itself a nod to some inner stirring. How you dress them is largely up to you. Typically, though, log décor is mindful of the walls. And while nobody will pigeonhole one log or corner treatment as being specific to any given style, certain building techniques and finishes can suggest a certain ambience and are, in fact, chosen for that reason. Rough-peeled and dark-stained trunks are often rustic and casual—popular in fishing cabins, boot-scootin' getaways, and Adirondack-style retreats. Traditional hand-hewn dovetail construction might assume historical proportions and be furnished accordingly with Early American

antiques and collectibles. Round, smooth-skinned walls with light finishes often have a flair for the contemporary. Contemporary, however, can mean almost anything, and logs aren't bound by any particular design criteria except, of course, their own compelling presence.

While designers disdain the concept of developing interior "themes," décor often flows in common currents of understanding. Often, we can point to one house and see the Wild West, then point to another and see Mission style or Arts & Crafts. Then again, we might only see "eclectic," where design is driven more by color and detail than by history or culture.

Apostles of the Arts & Crafts movement used stained glass to soften the harsh light emanating from that relatively new invention—electric lightbulbs. The idea was to re-create a gentler glow from days gone by. The same effect was also achieved with frosted and hand-painted shades like the one on this original Philip Handel lamp. The stained glass in the transom windows is not old, but the pattern and colors are characteristic of the period.

Log homes wear rustic and western tradition as easily as a cowboy wears his boots and rides old Paint. The décor is partly about history and heartfelt connections, but not entirely. People can't resist the infusion of color and character into a room. In Carol Gardner's homestead—a remake of an 1892 ranch house that once stood in the exact spot—a sense of history mingled with a hearty dose of levity for life sets the stage for décor that's characterized by horns, hides, wide plank floors, and colorful rustic furniture.

No matter how your home ends up, identify your point of inspiration early on. Is your log-home vision rooted in a nostalgic memory, someplace you've been, or the gratifying presence of a fish-filled brook and mountain vista? Will it be a showplace for family heirlooms, cherished antiques, or cabin collectibles? If it's a second home, will you abandon the formality of your other life, go hog-wild with color, or indulge your wildest dreams? Perhaps it's the wood and an abiding respect for nature that fuels your passion.

With a general sense of where your house is going, you can begin to narrow down your palette of colors and materials. Pick surfaces that support your vision and colors that complement it. The texture and tone of your walls,

FACING PAGE: The Gardners wanted the rebuilt fireplace to ride a little roughshod like those humble stacks of old. They hired Robin Ziniker to do the work, despite the fact that he plugged himself as "precision masonry." The stones were already a few feet high when Carol got her first peek. It was perfect—too perfect. Carol says she prescribed a bottle of rum, and a second try later, Robin got the idea! An old cooking pot hangs in front of the hearth and backyard pinecones fill a bear bowl carved in the Native American tradition of the Pacific Northwest.

LEFT: This home, says architect Mike Ryan, "is of its own time and place." Since they were not trying to evoke the past or mimic some other style, there were no particular design limitations or constraints. They drew on available resources and the talents of local craftspeople to create a home that suits the lifestyle and aesthetics of the owners. This living room is the heart of the house, and TV is okay. Instead of hiding the fact that there is one, they picked the most logical spot for viewing, then placed the set in a contemporary, leather-faced cabinet.

counters, floors, and cabinets will forge an outline for the story that unfolds around your furnishings, art, and accessories.

Narrowing down your choices can be overwhelming. Although your budget may dictate tile over granite or carpet over wood, the inspiration for slathering your kitchen cabinets in fire-engine red or papering a framed wall with a bold floral print can be as paralyzing as it is exciting. Certainly you can make a wrong turn, but if the fear of trying leaves you with a dull, neutral palette, your log house might lack the very qualities you desire most. If you haven't yet, this may be a good time to seek decorating advice. You can start with friends and log-home neighbors or local showrooms and design studios. Beyond that, personal expert advice can be a marvelous thing. Not only do professional decorators and designers have keen eyes and access to a huge array of resources, but they can help you make a tidy, gratifying package out of myriad loose ends that threaten to tie you up in knots.

Remember that a concept doesn't happen overnight. Log-home owners, in particular, like to let their visions simmer—sometimes for years—before they move forward with a plan or purchase. Typically, they'll have drawers and boxes full of clippings and a stack of design books on their shelves. Plenty of ideas and a basic understanding of log-house architecture are very good things. Custom log homes can be expensive. Not only can logs and the accompanying architecture be more costly than other forms of construction, but people also tend to select high-end finishes. Floors and counters of solid wood or natural stone and tile, custom-painted and hand-rubbed walls and cabinetry, rich durable fabrics—these are just some of the ways people imbue their homes with warmth and heart-tugging appeal.

Southwest tradition and Santa Fe styling are strongly remembered in this Colorado home where the owners loved the mixed look of adobe and log. From the Mexican Saltillo tiles on the floor to the sun-bleached skull over the handcrafted door, this home, built by artisan Steve Cappellucci, is a personalized expression of that indigenous architecture.

Reds and yellows pop against dark-stained, rough-hewn fir floors and treads in this campy retreat. A chenille couch, vibrant rugs, and coordinated kitchen cabinetry form a stream of color that flows through the entire house.

COLOR UP!

*W*ood is a beautiful thing, and log walls present a splendid textural backdrop for fields and forests full of color. From soft wheats and muted greens to the raw, pure reds, yellows, and blues of spring in bloom, log-home décor is often awash with the colors of nature. Logs soak up color like they soak up light, and if the mood and palette suit you, rooms can be pleasingly drenched in it. Other times, pops of bright color used sparingly but often and everywhere can unify a space and create flow among rooms that spill over into each other.

Color is the designer's most powerful and versatile tool. It can wake up a dark space, make a small space seem bigger, or cause a big space to seem more intimate and inviting. It can lull you into peaceful reflection or spur you into energetic or lighthearted exchange. Sometimes a little goes a long way, and a 10-by-12-foot wall of indigo will be a whole lot bluer than a 1-by-1-foot square of it.

Color often had symbolic meaning for indigenous peoples, and cultures are remembered in traditional mixes and patterns. Navajo rugs and textiles, for instance, are foundational in western and, frequently, log-cabin décor. For better or worse, color also has significance for the times. Who can forget the 1970s love affair with burnt orange and chocolate brown or the 1960s rollick with avocado and harvest gold? Beyond that, color has personal meaning and significance. By the time we can count the Crayolas™ in our crayon box, there are one or two we definitely like best. Colors are often said to "suit" us and our personalities. Interior designers can frequently learn something of their clients' tastes by observing the way they dress.

When you settle into the task of choosing color, look first to your vision, then to your logs, the size of your room, and the visual impact of your log walls. Three or four dark-stained walls often compel lighter, brighter furnishings or big splashes of intense color. Lustrous, honey-colored wood may prefer to speak for itself, requesting predominantly subtle earthy tones. Grayed and pickled finishes, if not historically motivated, might open the door to colors that are more contemporary or to a roomful of cool neutrals.

Next, you might think about your floors, doors, window trim, and perhaps some of your framed walls as well— repetitious elements carried from room to room. The colors and finishes you choose for your logs and these other

Light almond-stained logs form the basis for a monochromatic color scheme in this home. Sleek, sophisticated furnishings appeal to the owner's flair for the contemporary, while the logs speak their familiar language without being rustic or overbearing. The colorful tapestry over the fireplace creates a surprise diversion in the room.

TIP

Plow through a stack of magazines and clip out every picture that appeals to you—don't ask why, just cut. Later, when you look through your piles, there will quite often be threads of consistency. Telltale colors and patterns pop up time and again. Before you know it, you've got your starting point!—LORI B. SHEPARDSON, NORTH STAR DESIGN

Kids love color and whimsy. Let them help you pick their favorites for a room that will bring them joy. These snug, red-fringed, yellow-and-black-checked spreads are a perfect fit for cowboy-boot beds carved by Idaho artisan R. C. Hink. Bear cubs fashioned with a chain saw peek through the window of the children's second-floor balcony to add another measure of enchantment.

permanent features often form the basis for a palette that flows throughout the entire house. Although the character of each room may be different, consistency with some of these basic unifying surfaces will lend a sense of calm and harmony to your home environment. And once you make some of those initial decisions, you often have enough purpose and direction to make some more.

Sometimes your impetus may come from a cherished object that will live in a room, such as your favorite red-leather couch, a hand-stitched quilt, or the area rug you inherited from Grandma Pearl. Even an adored plate or ceramic vase can inspire a mixable-matchable palette that will set the tone for a room or a house.

Not buying into traditional log-house mind-sets, the architect and homeowners chose contemporary cabinetry then used the same teal green stain carried throughout the house via the trim. While the color is bold, it's not meant to be jolting. Built-in mahogany cabinets and rust-colored upholstery on the dining room chairs create a striking but harmonious mix. Cork tiles, popular in the 1950s, are used on the floors and finished with a durable polyurethane finish.

PATTERN AND TEXTURE IN THE WELL-SUNG ROOM

*P*attern is a vehicle for introducing and blending color. As with shades of individual colors, pattern and scale frequently go hand in hand. Like warm colors, large-scale patterns can cozy up a room, while on a small scale, prints tend to recede, making a small room feel larger. Mini-prints can get lost on an oversized sofa backed up against a log wall. But in other applications, they can also hint at texture and create a subtle background for lively geometric or floral prints.

Along with color and pattern, texture brings three-part harmony to a well-sung room. Logs have texture. Often they are juxtaposed with hard natural surfaces like stone and polished granite. Weighty fabrics, both tactile and durable, can match the warmth of logs and soften or counter the rawness of other harsh surfaces. Log homes are comfortable homes, and texture, introduced through fabric, can bear out that snug sense of leisure. Soft to the touch, chenilles invite you to curl up by the fire. Leather is about the most durable fabric you can have. It'll stand up to rivets and jeans and big-buckled belts.

This log home is built into a hill so a portion of the foundation extends above ground-level into the room. While decorator Penny Savoia-Shawback could have faced that part of the wall with matching log siding, she intro-duced color through a papered wainscoting.

Designer Terri DeMun mixes up a roomful of cabiny prints, plaids, stripes, and checks. This colorful mixing and matching is simple and very forgiving, says Terri. It's not so stylized that people are afraid to try it at home. Like certain foods, quilts, throws, pillows, and braided rugs are comforting, and you can use them to spiff up or change the look of an entire room.

FIRST-PICK FABRICS AND TEXTILES

Fabrics are building blocks of home décor. Mix and match them for comfort, mood, and impact. For a new look, re-cover a couch, throw a half dozen patterned pillows on a bed, or re-dress your windows. Fabrics can also be backed and used as wall coverings, much like paper but with more muscle. Coarse treatments and nubby textures are especially popular in log homes. Formal fabrics like silks and polished cottons are much less so. That may go double in high-altitude homes where silks will be the first to fade and rot under the merciless glare of the sun. Fading, however, is an issue with any fabric. While the dyes in some textiles and rugs will be more stable than in others, low-E glass and window dressings are often a must. Durability and feet-up comfortable are also high on the log-lover's list. Scotchgard, Fiber Sealing, or some other stain repellent applied by the manufacturer or after installation can mean less fuss and worry. Since quality and price vary tremendously among similar fabrics—be they leathers, cottons, or wools—you may need to shop around. Upholstery demands comfortable heavyweight fabrics, but a couch may need to stand up to more wear than a club chair or a padded hallway bench.

Leather

While greenhorns have been known to slide right off a shiny leather couch, the fabric can be tough as nails and entirely at home with logs. It's not all rough-and-tumble either. Leather comes in a variety of colors and varying degrees of softness and quality depending on the process of tanning and dying. Hard waxy hides are easy to clean and sometimes embossed with various designs that are typically western. Higher-grade leathers are softer and more comfortable. Suede is particularly soft but not as rugged as other treatments. It's not as water-repellent either so it's much more difficult to clean. Multipurposed, leather

Light-colored decking brightens up dramatic timber-framed ceilings in this home furnished by owner/designer Susie Moreland. Susie used crown molding and wallpaper to split the tall walls and create a comfortable scale. Wanting a more feminine European feel over something western, she chose paper with English prints. For consistency, a neutral shade of taupe was used on the upper portion of the walls and repeated on all the woodwork, cabinetry, and trim throughout the house. A section of the inexpensive character-grade maple floor is sponge-painted with diamonds to mimic a large area rug.

There are rules of thumb when it comes to choosing pattern and color. Dark warm colors and large-scale patterns can dwarf a small room. But, says designer Char Thompson, why not let a small room just feel small and draw you in? While she did pick a dense small-scale print over something larger for the powder room, the idea was to create an inviting retreat—not to enlarge and brighten the space. Fossil-imprinted countertops, corkscrew willow, and Char's simple dried arrangement under the sink liken this little room to a shady garden nook.

LEFT: Most any tightly woven fabric can be backed and used like wallpaper. The homeowner picked a Ralph Lauren print for her bedroom and carried it to the log wall, where it is carefully scribed around the notch work. The fireplace beyond the French doors was faux-painted to soften stark plaster walls and resemble limestone.

In this mountain home, the colors had to be vibrant, warm, and pretty—yet rustic, says designer Beth Slifer. English chintz pillows and a plaid rag rug have country overtones, but it's not cute like gingham and bows. The powerful architecture, rich brown leather, and blocky 500-pound coffee table help see to that.

RIGHT: Lofts and dormered spaces make wonderful tuck-away rooms for guests and children. Often set apart from the rest of the house, there may be more opportunity to play with color and pattern. In this bedroom niche, a showy green-and-red-trimmed carpet opens the door to flashy pattern and color.

is also great for such things as cornice boards, tooled paneling, and desktops. Cowhides—complete with hair, spots, and brands—are fun to throw on the floor, carve up for pillows, or tack down on firm benches and side chairs.

Ultrasuede®

This synthetic polyester blend looks and feels like real animal suede but is machine washable and dryable. It comes in dozens of colors and patterns. Though developed for upholstery, it is best used on accessories and secondary pieces rather than on the family's jump-about sofa.

Wool

"Dyed in the wool" means genuine. Natural, durable, versatile wools are used for everything from carpet to drapes.

While some weaves can be on the prickly side, most really aren't. Instead, offering log-home warmth and texture, they are often used for upholstery. Some designers adore wool drapes, but softer, nicely hanging wools can be very expensive and difficult to clean. Operable drapes eat up fabric, and it can take yards to make a single eighteen-inch panel. Pure wool carpets can be plush and wonderful, but less-expensive wool blends may be more resistant to stains or better suited to the comings and goings of hikers and skiers.

Vintage blankets

Old wool Pendletons and cotton Beacon blankets deliver a hearty dose of color, pattern, and western charm. People can't resist using them for chair and sofa cushions, but they don't wear particularly

Soft distressed-leather couches and Navaho weavings were a logical fit in this western great room designed to entertain and showcase the owner's extensive collection of art and sculpture. Deciding how to finish the entryway, however, took a little more chin scratching. After a number of brainstorming sessions and living with the plywood framework for several weeks, the owners and their decorator, Andrea Lawrence Wood, hit on the idea of tooled leather. It took leather-artisan Rick Montanari many months to do the archway, several cornice boards over the windows, and counters for the office.

MORE THAN ONE WAY TO WEAR A BLANKET

- Hang your trade blankets over open ceiling beams or railings.
- Spread one over a coffee table or use as a tablecloth in the dining room.
- Drape over the corner of an extra-wide mantel and place decorative objects on top.
- Tack one on a log wall and hang a picture or two over that, or use your blanket as a backdrop on the wall behind a tableful of western collectibles.
- Fill display cupboards or oversized baskets with folded blankets.
- Hang a series of blankets from the rungs of a ladder leaning against a wall.
- Use as throws over sofas, chairs, beds, and headboards.
- Hang a blanket behind your bed in lieu of a headboard.

In old western movies, nearly every horse you see is saddled with a wool Pendleton or cotton Beacon blanket. Patterned from Native American designs, this vintage Pendleton-blanket collection from the 1920s and up adds zippy western color in a log home.

well, especially if they're old and worn to begin with. If it matters, try them on pillows or chair backs instead, or shop for new look-alike materials specially designed for sitting. Since blankets were never intended to be used for upholstery, a knit backing is essential to shore them up for the kind of rubbing and scooching that happens when you sit. In other instances, think about using vintage blankets as side panels for draperies, or pair one with a plastic liner to curtain a shower.

Kilim and other old rugs

Kilim textiles are boldly patterned flat-weave rugs crafted by tribal people living in Turkey and Afghanistan. Richly textured, kilim and other recycled rugs

make great rugs—but they can also be cut up for pillows or used for seat cushions, benches, and ottomans. They are rarely used for lounging since the material is scratchy and coarse. Not only that, the vigorous kilim patterns can be overpowering in large doses.

Jute and natural grasses

Jute, or sisal, is a stiff fibrous plant that is commonly woven into rugs. While durable, it stains easily and can't be readily cleaned. Prevention is the key, and sisal rugs are treated with stain repellents after they're installed. Most designers won't use them in the kitchen or bath, but they work well in bedrooms or other low-traffic areas. Woven grass

Along with hunky masculine furniture, homeowner Elizabeth Tierney is drawn to leather, wool, stone, and metal—natural, durable materials intended to last. When her feminine side takes over, she uses lace and gentler fabrics to soften the room. Lace draped from railroad spikes pounded into the wall and woven-grass shades from the Philippines dress the doors. More lace hangs from decorative ironwork over the bed. The tiger, a family heirloom, adds another dimension of pattern to the roomscape.

Desiring drama but not wanting the fabrics to upstage the materials in this wood and timber-framed home, the designer chose subtle shades for most of the furnishings, including the soft chenille on the sofa. For warmth and contrast, rich reds are used in small doses throughout the house. Since full draperies are expensive and unnecessary with motorized duette shades, the designer chose an abbreviated iron rod and drapery panel. A leaf-shaped finial adds the final poetic touch.

shades make fabulous semitransparent window shades. Light filters through lowered blinds that look wonderful when they're down. Other grasses and fibers, including bamboo, coconut, and sea grass, can be used on walls, floors, or even ceilings. While these organic materials are generally very durable, high humidity or extreme dryness may impact function and wear. Shop for quality and pick a manufacturer that will stand behind its product.

Chenille

Everyone loves the luscious enveloping quality of chenille. In French, chenille means "caterpillar," which suits this soft fuzzy pile woven from a variety of materials that include manmade fibers, wool, cotton, and even silk. There are hundreds of different kinds of chenilles with varying degrees of quality and durability. While some aren't easily bothered by wet-nosed pets, cat claws, or sticky candy, others are far more fragile. Although not as dressy as velvet or mohair, chenille is soft, textured, and available in a stunning array of colors and patterns. Depending on the weight of the fabric, chenilles are suitable for couches and chairs, pillows, throws, and sometimes even draperies. The higher the quality, the more likely a chenille will resist crushing and flattening with long-term use.

Linen

Woven from flax, linen has great natural texture. It's wrinkly, of course, but holds up well and can make wonderful draperies. It softens over time. For a little less rumple, try a linen blend.

Cotton

It's the everything, everywhere fabric! Natural and extremely versatile, cotton comes in a dazzling array of colors and a multitude of weaves, from wispy to upholstery-weight durable. Cut up western cotton scarves for pillows. Use a row of brightly colored dishtowels for whimsical country-kitchen valances. Turn beautiful cotton sheets into shower curtains, window treatments, or inexpensive duvet covers.

The walls of this bathroom were not painted. Instead, plaster tinged with color was layered on for a textured finish reminiscent of aged Italian stucco. Faux painters frequently try to re-create this fabulous timeworn effect on less-expensive sheet-rocked and textured surfaces. The pale ochre in custom tiles from Pratt & Larson served as inspiration for the color on the walls.

THE POWER OF PAINT

Never underestimate the power of paint—or the possibilities. While solid-colored walls will never go out of style, there are dozens of ways to add depth and texture alongside the color. From stenciling and the notion of hand-painted wallpaper to myriad faux finishes, paint is the proverbial jack-of-all-trades. Some of the techniques are ages old. Cavemen, of course, painted pictures on their walls, and as early as the sixth century B.C., artists in the ancient city of Pompeii used tromp l'oeil—the technique of creating three-dimensional pictures that can look so real you want to reach out and touch them.

Color should be fun! Experts insist that it can create feelings of joy and transform your life. Canary yellow walls with blue trim do just that in this unpretentious cordwood home built from the ground up by owners Tom and Florence Blanchard. And if they ever tire of it, they'll think nothing of repainting.

BAG IT!

Now what? You've been to the paint store, the tile house, the rug mart, and the fabric place. You've pawed through catalogs and carted home sample books. Finally you're getting somewhere. This may be the time to organize your chips, paper patterns, and swatches on sample boards, in binders, or, better yet, how 'bout baggies?

Try filling big plastic bags with the goods, one for each room. You can include clippings from magazines, snapshots of special items you might purchase, and notes with various room measurements. Baggies squash down, travel well, and make it easy to swap out one sample or idea for another.

This homeowner is a great fan of Colombian artist Fernando Botero, but the last time she came across one of his original paintings, it was priced at nearly half a million dollars. While she couldn't bring it home, she did give her artist friend Ellen Gladis a book featuring his work, and asked her to have some like-minded fun on the laundry-room wall.

BELOW: Light switches blend like chameleons with logs and natural-stone tiles. Painted by Karen Jones, faux finishes like these offer possibilities that are extensive.

Today, accomplished artists, along with do-it-yourselfers, make use of imagination and a plethora of tools that include everything from sea sponges and cellophane to feathers and hairbrushes. Sometimes, they sponge, rag, and comb wet paint on and off objects or walls. Other times, painted surfaces impersonate marble, limestone, wood, or rusty metal. Crackled and hand-rubbed finishes can add a hundred years to an old hutch or a cabinet door. Faux finishes on walls can be moody and romantic with effects that change or deepen with sunlight and lamplight.

Paint, whether solid-colored or something more exotic, is always affected by the amount and quality of light in a room. The differences can sometimes be striking. A soft sage, for instance, can go gray, or creams can feel yellow. Before you settle on a paint or finish, observe a sample in its anticipated resting place throughout the day and night. The very best way is to see something painted directly onto the wall, but if that's not possible, a 1-by-2-foot or 2-by-2-foot square will tell you more than a pint-size chip that fits in the palm of your hand.

Beyond this kitchen, a wraparound screened-in porch provides delightful bug-free dining in summer but reduces the amount of natural light coming into the room. Cheery fabrics and gaily painted tiles brighten up the space. The cabinetry was designed to look more like furniture, and the oxidized blue-green paint is derived from colors in the pear-print balloon valances. Crown molding on the cabinets made it easy to conceal lights aimed at the ceiling. Morgan's Fine Finishing did the painting and staining on the cabinetry, floors, and trim.

FACT

Milk paint was historically made with milk proteins, quicklime, and earth pigments. It was used by early American colonists and Shakers, but the formulas date back to ancient Egypt. Durable, long-lasting, nontoxic, and user friendly, milk paint is still available. Use it to authenticate the look of antique furniture, historic houses, and stenciled floors. —THE OLD FASHIONED MILK PAINT COMPANY INC., www.milkpaint.com

Worn-out colors along with open shelving and cabinet doors faced with chicken wire take the shine out of a new kitchen and give it farmhouse appeal. If you want to keep dishes low to the floor, don't overlook the curiosity factor of toddlers and pets.

BOTTOM: Bookshelves line two walls from floor to ceiling in Jim and Alison Luckman's guest space above the garage. Alison painted the walls with milk-paint special-ordered through the mail. The pigment comes dry and is mixed with water at the time of use. Unlike regular paint, the finish is chalky and old-fash-ioned. Milk-paint stenciling along with a cowboy bed and rawhide lampshade from New West western-up the little bedroom beyond.

Artist V. Patrick writes, "Red is a power color. Red is warm and Western winters are long and cold." True enough, red is both powerful and warm in this family room where a bold entertainment center built by Tribes sets the tone. The color overflows into comfortable chairs and the horse painting by Susan Hertel. A coffered ceiling adds another layer of texture, pattern, and light.

Because faux finishes can be warm and moody, particularly in log homes, consider the effects of artificial lighting. Lights with dimmers let you play with color and take full advantage of the range of looks one wall can offer.

The cost for specialized finishes varies dramatically depending on the complexity of the process and degree of skill that's required. Artists may charge by the job or by the square foot, with an additional expense added for each color used. One-of-a-kind faux finishes will certainly be more expensive than plain paint but sometimes cost less than wallpaper.

From the do-it-yourselfer's point of view, paint is freeing and fun. It's not so complicated that you can't tackle a wall if you're so inclined. Faux finishes can require more time and skill, but some of the techniques are relatively simple to learn. And paint is forgiving. If you really blow it, you can layer on some primer and begin again. Immerse yourself in the art and craft of faux techniques at www.fauxlikeapro.com.

"There is something infinitely healing in the repeated refrains of nature."—Rachel Carson

THE NATURAL SURFACE

Log homes are steeped in a timeless sense of permanence. Unabashedly knit to nature, we instinctively want to pair them with kindred materials: stone, granite, more wood, earth-inspired tiles. Such materials are favorites for log-cabin floors, countertops, tubs, showers—all the various hard surfaces that map out space and create flow and transition, changing the page from one room to the next. Sometimes they add trendsetting texture and color. Other times, they merely support flavorful furnishings.

When choosing hard-surface materials, the usual questions of style, function, use, and budget get filtered through our subjective nets of purpose and desire. Sometimes, function alone can help narrow the field. Kids, pets, and relaxed living may steer you clear of light-colored carpets or point you to surfaces that are more durable and easily maintained. Radiant-heat floors work best with toppings such as stone, brick, or poured concrete. A kitchen gourmet might want to work in a section of butcher-block countertop along with granite, while a family with small children might avoid unforgiving stone floors in the kitchen and rec room.

This home is a mingling of those natural materials that are so utterly at home with logs. Each element, from the river-rock fireplace and the wood and slate floors to the granite and natural-tile countertops, adds unique texture and form to this versified palette. Slate, characterized by uneven layered surfaces, makes for better floors than it does countertops, since food bacteria can hide in hard-to-clean clefts. Impregnating sealers are often used to waterproof tiles and help prevent them from scuffing. Most masons recommend that slate be used indoors rather than on outdoor patios, particularly in cold climates.

Built with huge logs by A Place in the Sun Log Homes, this house has settled several inches over time. Anticipating that in advance, the builders set the posts on adjustable jacks beneath the floors. Since logs will shrink from side to side rather than end to end, those posts have to be lowered when the walls of a house settle. Since the posts must be permitted to slide free of the floor, strips of Douglas fir butt up against the logs but do not extend underneath them in the usual manner. The floors were left natural and sealed with a water-based clear-coat finish.

UNDER YOUR FEET

The installation techniques for floors in log homes are much the same as for those in other forms of construction, with a few likely exceptions. New homes will creak and yawn a bit as they settle into the task of being a house. Log homes do that even more, so floors should be laid with shrinking and settling in mind. For instance, logs can actually pull away from the floor over time. Consequently, flooring doesn't stop at the edge of a wall but is actually tucked back under the logs. Since logs are not straight, installing baseboards can be difficult or time-consuming. Most often, they simply aren't used. Instead, gaps between the floor and wall will often be sealed with a flexible bead of chink or caulk.

RADIANT HEAT: WALKING ON (WARM!) WATER

Radiant in-floor heat is a clean, quiet, and increasingly popular way to heat log homes. Why? For one thing, you don't have to worry about concealing extensive ductwork amidst log walls (unless, of course, your climate also demands air-conditioning). For another, the mass and thermal properties of logs cause warm air to move slowly through the walls. Once logs warm up, they stay that way and do a super job of keeping the air temperature constant and comfortable. Initially, the system will cost more to install, but if you plan on living in your home for a long time, lower operating costs may even out the bill within a few years. Your home will also take longer to warm when you first turn up the thermostat, but you have the added advantage of separating spaces into zones that can be conveniently regulated independent of one another. You can't easily do that with forced-air systems unless you add a second furnace.

Sometimes, an oversized glass-filled room in a cold-climate home will require a secondary source of heat. To find out, a mechanical engineer may need to do the math before you send your plans out to bid with heating contractors. Heat recovery and ventilation systems are common additions too, since they refresh stale air inside a well-sealed home and may help prevent the harmful buildup of radon gas that can be a problem in some regions around the country.

When you choose radiant heat, certain floors will be more practical than others. Materials such as stone, concrete, tile, and brick work best. Typically cold to the touch, they will feel as sun-warmed as a backyard patio on a new spring day. And unlike some insulating carpets, those dense, solid surfaces allow heat to move readily through them into a room. Carpeting can be used over radiant slabs, but you want to select pads and materials with low insulative values that won't trap the heat.

Wood flooring works well too, despite some sentiment to the contrary. It must, however, be properly installed. To prevent the wood from shrinking, the concrete subfloor must be completely dry and the wood thoroughly acclimated to the climate inside a home, sometimes for several weeks before it's laid down. Certain species of wood are more stable than others, and narrow boards or strips will expand and contract less than wider planks. Quartersawn material or

A band of quartzite, better known in the Mountain West as oakley stone, meanders around the perimeter of the living room before widening into a path that leads to an outdoor deck. Multicolored, character-grade hickory wood is laid around the stone. Both materials are placed atop hydronic radiant-heat floors, but each required a different method of installation. Varying thicknesses of stone are laid in a mud bed while the wood is nailed down to a layer of plywood that in turn rests on lightweight concrete. Water-filled tubing is laced throughout the entire floor.

laminated wood flooring will also be more stable than traditional sawn boards or natural wood.

Acid-stained or imprinted concrete flooring is a logical and often economical fit with radiant heat since concrete is already in use as the substrate for hot-water tubing woven through the floor. Extra measures will be taken to prevent the slab from cracking as it dries out, and the final layer of concrete will be specially reinforced throughout.

As with concrete, tile, slate, and stone do an excellent job of banking the heat and radiating it evenly into a room. While there are different methods of installing these materials, one important goal is to prevent cracks in the subfloor from transferring to the finished surface. Tile and stone are rarely set

directly on top of the slab since fractures—even in well-cured concrete—can lead to subtle movement that will damage the finished floor. Rubber mats or isolation membranes placed between the two surfaces are one way to prevent this from happening. Flexible grouts are also used for a little more give and take between the tiles.

Many people get their first glimpse of log construction in famous lodges scattered throughout America's national parks and destination resorts. Designed by Ruscitto/Latham/Blanton, the River Run Ski Lodge in Sun Valley, Idaho, has turned a few heads with its massive logs and upscale finishes. Boldly patterned wall-to-wall carpet laid atop radiant-heat floors is refined and elegant. The floral pattern is large so it doesn't get lost or disappear in this great space. While the lodge is much larger than any great room, scale is an important concept in the selection of patterned carpets or fabrics.

WONDERFUL WOOD

Traces of time suspended in rivers of swirling grain—no two pieces of wood are quite the same. Whether laid down for a floor or a counter or used for cabinetry and paneling, each tree—each unique species of wood—will distinguish itself in different ways. Strength, stability, appearance, and stainability may endear one wood over another in home décor. Spoken of as hardwoods or softwoods, there are many different species of wood and finishes to choose from.

Softwoods such as pine and fir come from coniferous or evergreen trees. While hardwoods aren't consistently "hard," softwoods do tend to dent, scratch, and mar more easily than many types of deciduous trees, including oak and maple. Pine is very soft and most likely to be used in casual surroundings where scrapes and nicks are chalked up to comfortable living or memorable events. Pine doesn't always stain evenly and may need to be treated with a wood conditioner before color is applied.

Recycled American chestnut (virtually eliminated in North America by the chestnut blight in the first decades of the 1900s) is a rich deep brown. You wouldn't choose it for light-colored floors or cabinets, but use a dark stain and it can be positively elegant. Maple, on the other hand, is a durable close-grained wood that doesn't stain well. Finish it with a transparent coat of wax for a natural-wood countertop, or seal it with bullet-proof clear coat for a light and pretty floor. White oak, another favorite hardwood, wears well enough for stair treads and is often finished in golden tones.

The list goes on from there and gets even longer if you consider exotic woods imported from around the globe. Conscientious homebuyers, however, may want to avoid endangered tropical hardwoods as well as vanishing indigenous old-growth species. While a "don't ask, don't tell" policy sometimes prevails in the United States, there are environmentally responsible companies, such as the California-based distributor EcoTimber, that will provide you with beautiful products certified to be harvested in sustainable ways.

When selecting woods for floors and accompanying trim work, doors, or paneling, Matt Morgan of Morgan's Fine Finishing advises people to choose woods that are "color friendly" with the ultimate finish they have in mind. In other words, think color first then choose a wood that can go there with you. Don't try to turn a chestnut into a maple or a maple into a chestnut. You should also be aware that, like fabric, wood can be light-sensitive and is subject to UV degradation, some varieties more

Paint adds color and character while hiding a myriad of sins. It's ideal for inexpensive or plain wood floors that surface during a remodel after the carpet comes up. Stencil and paint a faux area rug on a living room floor or full-size game boards in a child's bedroom or play area. Big checkerboard patterns are fun in a foyer, and if you keep it simple, you don't have to be an artist to pull it off.

so than others. Cherry and alder, for instance, discolor quickly in bright sunlight. Similarly, light or transparent stains may afford less protection than solid-body stains with lots of pigment. Think about the exposure of each room, and ask about the properties, durability, and recommended upkeep for the various woods and finishes you plan to live with.

On a floor, wood typically costs more than carpet and is often comparable to or less than tile. But time tells all. Wood cleans easier than carpet and usually outlasts it. And while the jury may still be out, people generally believe that wood is also easier to maintain than tile floors and countertops (especially those with small squares and lots of grout).

By combining colorfast woods with proper installation, good protective finishes, and standard upkeep, you can keep your surfaces beautiful for years and years. The experts recommend that a new wood floor get a maintenance coat

Not a single log or stick of wood was stained in this post-and-beam house built by its owner, Randy Hermann, and Montana craftsman Walt Smith. A clear natural-oil finish was used on the logs and a durable Swedish Glitsa finish coats the fir flooring of this sunlit passage. Time and exposure have also contributed to the amber glow of the logs, walls, and floor.

professionally applied after one year and again three to five years later. Beyond that, window coverings can knock back harmful UV radiation, and well-placed area rugs in high traffic zones can prevent over-wear in your entries and hallways. As for the rest of it, Mom already told you: wipe your feet, and don't let water sit on the floor. This is especially true in bathrooms and kitchens where water will splash about and settle into corners when you're not even looking. The maintenance requirements vary for wood with different finishes, so it's always best to check with your installer or follow the procedures suggested by the finish manufacturer.

LEFT: Pat Millington and her former husband Dick built their ranch house from a log package purchased back in 1973. Since then, Pat has updated some, remodeled a lot, and filled her home to the brim with cherished eclectic treasures that include everything from her Italian grandmother's inlaid ivory bench to original Stickley chairs, a welded horse sculpture by Deborah Butterfield, and a 1911 birch-bark canoe perched in the rafters. Her commercial oak flooring came pre-finished from the factory, but Pat never liked the color. Some time ago she sanded it down to bare wood, then used a clear finish to let the natural grain shine through.

BELOW: Wood ends lopped from milled two-by-fours make floors akin to brick. Owner-builder Steve Abbey had seen these floors in wineries but did not consider using them in his home until he scored on a load for a buck at a hometown auction. He installed them himself then sealed them with verathane that darkened the wood considerably. (Some of his dinky toys date back to Waterloo, and, as the story goes, Napoleon actually used these very toys while mapping out military strategy in his tent.)

WHAT'S ON THAT FLOOR?

You can't properly care for an old wood floor if you don't know what's on it. To find out if it's finished with wax, shellac, varnish, or a hard-coat surface finish, try scraping the wood with a coin. If the finish flakes, it's probably shellac or varnish. The chances of that are especially good if the floor was installed or last serviced before the mid-1960s since neither product is used much for flooring anymore. Refinishing will require sanding down to bare wood.

If the finish is wax, white spots will appear within ten minutes of dripping two droplets of water onto the floor. Remove the spots by gently rubbing them with wax-dampened steel wool (#000). If neither spots nor flakes come to bear, your floor has a surface finish and should be maintained accordingly. For more information, see www.woodfloorsonline.com.

This functional stainless-steel range melds high-tech with other natural surfaces, including a stone backsplash and a wood-and-stucco vent hood.

RIGHT: Since natural stone is used on the kitchen counters, a wood-topped island provides an alternative surface for prepping food. With storage at one end and seating on the other three sides, this central station becomes a gathering spot for family and friends. Slide the stools in underneath, and several cooks can hurry around the kitchen. Multipurpose islands are ever popular, but if you include seating, make sure you have enough room to pass behind the stools when they're pulled out into the room.

CONCRETE EVIDENCE

If you hear the words "concrete floor-ing" and picture the cracked and oil-stained slab in your garage, think again. Concrete floors are among the most intriguing developments for residential construction in recent years. And it doesn't stop at floors. Concrete special-ists are using it for countertops, showers, tubs, fireplaces, architectural features, and outdoor benches. They come in a rich variety of colors and textures: sometimes smooth and acid-stained, other times enhanced with thin coatings

Howard and Mischa Leendertsen's stone-and-timber cottage was first conceived as a small gatehouse for what was to be a much-larger estate. When that project failed to materialize, the Leendertsens bought the empty shell. Together with architect Jim McLaughlin and decorator Lori Shepardson, the cottage was enlarged and redesigned with French-country appeal. The fireplace is faced with the same type of sandstone used for the exterior walls, and the mantel surround is precast concrete with a faux-crackle limestone finish. The sconce on the wall is made from carved semiopaque alabaster.

of cement. And since the fluidity of wet cement makes it so mold-able, experts can imprint or shape the material into floors or out-door patios that resemble tile, flagstone, or even brick.

Acid staining has been popular for about a decade but possibly made its first notable mark in the 1920s when the designers of Yosemite National Park Lodge in California used it there. The process

gives the concrete an aqueous, mottled appearance. The colors are somewhat limited to shades that include black, caramel or reddish browns, various greens, and a few blue tones. Cement coatings are a little more like paint. A very thin layer is applied on top of the floor with a trowel. Most any color can be used, and a colored coating can be troweled over a different shade of flooring for a variety of effects.

While concrete floors can be more expensive than wood, they often cost less than tile and stone floors, especially when you consider the added labor, material expense, and the fact that stone and tile must generally be laid on top of concrete to begin with. Countertops may cost more since they are more difficult to do and special frames have to be built on top of the cabinetry. As a counter, concrete is most likely to be smooth and

seamless. In the kitchen, however, concrete can blunt a sharp knife, so think about using cutting boards or butcher blocks.

For all practical purposes, the color in concrete is permanent and nonfading. With normal use and proper maintenance, it should not be necessary to reseal or recolor it. Initially, however, a well-sealed surface is key. If you have three dogs, two cleat-wearing kids, and a shoes-on policy indoors, you might pick a solvent-based epoxy sealant for a floor instead of a water-based acrylic. Always avoid harsh cleaning products that might damage the finish. Water and mild soap are all you really need. Also, be aware that concrete floors can scuff. Sometimes that's desirable, but if not, you'll want to be a little careful when you move furniture around.

Pine strips forming a gridwork around large squares of concrete are decorative, but gridding the floor also helps prevent cracks from developing on the surface. Muriatic acid (not to be confused with acid staining) was used first to clean the concrete and make it a bit more porous. The mottled uneven finish was produced intentionally with different coats of a tinted sealant. Gridding is just one of many ways to style a concrete floor, and other materials such as copper or tin-wrapped boards could replace the pine for a different look.

NATURAL STONE

Natural stone takes you at once to the river or slope or outdoor place distinctly marked by time and shaped by region. Fossil-imprinted, ablaze with lichen, or veined and colored with the raw, pure strokes of nature, the connection is often immediate, especially inside a log home. With proper sealants, stone—including granites, slates, marbles, limestones, and others—makes fabulous floors and countertops. Natural stone is water-resistant and exceptionally durable. However, it is also as hard and unforgiving inside as it is outside, and can be noisy to walk on and cold underfoot unless combined with radiant-heat floors.

Stone is naturally porous and sometimes rough and uneven. If you use it for counters or walls in the kitchen or bath, consider its potential for staining and prospects for cleaning. Smooth surfaces won't give gunk a place to hide. The hardness of a given stone may also make one type of material a better candidate for some areas of a home than others. Limestone and sandstone, for instance, are softer and easily gouged. Virtually all natural stone surfaces should be sealed then resealed periodically—sometimes every few years, other times every few months. While home-owners can often do this chore themselves, the frequency of recommended upkeep might sway them one way or the other. To find out more on the web, check out the stone industry's home page at www.natural-stone.com.

Intrigued by European mosaics and wanting a forgiving method of laying stone, home-owner Michael Rudigoz pieced together chunks and chips of tumbled marble for his wine cellar floor. The tiles were leftovers from another project. Having no previous experience, Michael didn't find the task difficult—only time-consuming.

LEFT: A colorful border delineates a section of this tumbled marble floor much like an area rug would. This foyer was created when the Leendertsens enclosed the open area between their small stone-walled, timber-framed cottage and matching garage. The floors are durable enough for ski boots but also make a beautiful backdrop for entertaining, since the new entry doubles as a formal dining area. In the adjacent living room, the area rug was custom made with a leafy border borrowed from the Jacquard chenille fabric used on the sofa.

BELOW: The fleur-de-lis is a recurring theme in the Leendertsen home. In this bathroom, the small iris mosaics were hand-pieced into limestone tiles around the tub and shower. Lei's Custom Tiles, a small father-and-son business, did the handiwork onsite using pieces of the same granite installed on the bathroom vanity. The color variations in the large squares of French limestone occur naturally. The tiles were randomly arranged and closely set with nearly invisible lines of grout.

MEDLEY OF TILES

Tile stores hold the same allure for me now as the candy counter did when I was a kid. Then, the possibilities seemed nearly endless and the decisions were often agonizing. I suppose it helped that I only had fifty cents and not a dollar—although I'm certain the reality of my good fortune escaped me at the time.

Unlike stone, ceramic tiles are made from fire-hardened clay. They can be textured, sculpted, and cut into a variety of geometric shapes. Either glazed or unglazed, they come in an extraordinary range of colors, patterns, and designs. Unglazed tiles, such as terra-cotta, have a matte finish, are porous, and need to be sealed like natural stone to prevent staining. Glazing is a covering or sealant applied to the tile when it's fired. The finishes can be shiny, matte, or anything in between. Porcelain tiles, made from finer clays fired to higher temperature, are the most durable tiles you can buy.

Found all over the world, granite comes in more than 150 different colors and varieties. It is one of the densest stones you can buy and is often the most expensive. In the owner's "dream kitchen," they used a solid granite slab with sculpted edges on their island and matching but less-expensive tiles on the countertops. Above the stove, there is a special tap for filling pots and a forest scene crafted with specialty tiles from Water-works in San Francisco.

Unlike ceramic tiles that rarely exceed sixteen or twenty-four inches square, natural stone comes in a variety of sizes, dimensioned depending on the material. Masons might work with small chips, dimensioned squares, large and odd-shaped pieces, or giant slabs straight from the quarry. This kitchen island combines big lichen-covered chunks of stone with stacks of flat fractured rock. While lichen wouldn't wear well on the floor, stones with this colorful growth are great for vertical surfaces like walls, fireplaces, and foundation fronts.

RIGHT: Clay tiles like Mexican Saltillos are relatively inexpensive compared to other tiles. However, they can drink up sealer and may need to have it reapplied more often. Area rugs add warmth and comfort to the floor, but they are also important in décor. They define conversation areas and set up pathways through the house. When purchasing rugs, check for directional patterns or central medallions that might impact their positioning in a room. While it may not be desirable to mix and match styles, at other times, a combination of oriental rugs, Turkish kilims, or Native American textiles works just fine.

BELOW: Tiles can be custom-designed to fit most any criteria. Artists can create an entire mural for a shower wall or use a few individual tiles for accent. Intricate designs, raised borders and special-order materials will be more expensive than field tiles, but sometimes it only takes a few key tiles to change the face of an entire room.

Slate is a sedimentary
stone that comes in more
colors than you might
imagine. Grays and blacks
are common, but sunset
red, pinkish hues, and
blue-grays are among the
possibilities. Many of those
colorful tones are displayed
on these slate-tiled walls.

Centrally located and visible from the living, dining, and family rooms, this kitchen is literally the heart of the home. Its owners and designer Kelly Simpson wanted it to be light and happy. For the island and counters they chose a background field of irregular hand-cut ceramic tiles punctuated with a mix of decorative greens and accent strip tiles. A soft faux finish on the walls and distressed knotty-alder cabinets with imperfect antique-glass doors contribute an aged and mellow presence to the room. Peruse www.ceramic-tile.com for lists and links related to tile.

RUGS AND CARPETS

In general, wall-to-wall carpeting is used more often in a log-home bedroom than in a family or living area, but that doesn't mean that nubby neutrals or vividly patterned coverings won't be the exception. Sometimes, homeowners will choose a neutral base carpet then use decorative area rugs on top. To prevent your rugs from bunching up, select lower-piled carpets and purchase special pads designed to minimize that problem.

Tile is as versatile as it is beautiful. Sugar-pine paneling and a fireplace framed in a blue-and-white Dutch motif lend formality to this cozy den. Porcelain tile is a good choice for a fireplace hearth since it will be less prone to chipping than other ceramic products.

Character COUNTS

Paint and a twig-work makeover transform cheap secondhand cabinets into respectable cabin fare. Above the recycled apron sink, homeowner/artist Marti Fulton portrays the view out her faux window. Marti has four versions of the same painting and trades them out with the seasons.

FROM HEART TO HOME

*I*n the journey from heart to home, we alternately scan the horizon and stop to gather small curiosities strewn along our path. Whether building new or remaking the old, our perspective zooms in and out, back and forth, between our larger vision of the house to smaller notions of individual rooms filled with beautiful, curious, and necessary things. From the bookshelf to the bookend and the lighting fixture to the switch plate, each additional element has the potential to turn a head, bring a smile, or inspire a question. So it is that we imbue our homes with character—adding mementos from our past, building collections, and making way for imagination and new discoveries. In this section we look at a few of the infinite ways that log-home owners personalize their cabins, decks, and gardens through the pleasures of new, old, collectible, and recycled objects and trimmings.

A clay pot full of twiggy pencils—sometimes the littlest things can usher in surprise and delight.

LEFT: Hinges, knobs, doorstops, and switch-plate covers—these are just a few examples of small and easy-to-overlook necessities in home décor. Birch-bark papering and rawhide trim make this one unique.

"What makes a place special is the way it buries itself inside the heart."——*Richard Nelson,* The Island Within

FACING PAGE: The owner describes her ironwork railings and door as being open, European, and not ho-hum. Both the rails and door leading down to the wine cellar were constructed from precast pieces purchased from various catalogs.

ABOVE: This 1930s cabin was falling down when its owner, Julie Stein, reclaimed it from a forest full of wild critters who had made it their home. Slung over a curtain rod, a rodeo scarf picked up on one of Julie's countless junking expeditions to the Blue Ridge Mountains adds to her casual but spirited décor.

The hearth is as much a part of cabin mystique as the logs are. It is a focal point and a gathering spot. Fire screens, both decorative and personal, often relate bits and pieces of a home's history. Here, a pair of falcons alight on matching andirons while a third stands watch on glass and metal doors crafted by Idaho metalworker Mark Sheehan. This home's namesake is "The Falcon's Nest"—that's where the story begins . . .

Before you meet homeowner Carol Gardner, you're likely to get a big sloppy kiss from her roly-poly bulldog, Zelda, the up-and-coming greeting-card diva. Along with Zelda, a Texas horned chair discovered in the want ads and an old one-armed bandit from the Slot Closet in Portland reflect Carol's lighthearted approach to both life and western décor.

BELOW: In the American Southwest, poles or branches called *latillas* were used in the construction of early adobe dwellings. Latillas are strongly reminiscent of that traditional architecture and are commonly used in shutters and doors or to line ceilings and roof overhangs.

ABOVE: Using dovetail joinery, Oregon craftsman Ed Adams treated these stairs like a piece of fine furniture. And, like fine furniture, these hand-worked treads become an eye-catching element of this cabin's décor.

When Mark and Patrice Cole built a master bedroom addition to their sawn-log cabin, they relegated most of the logs to the outside. The spirit of the place, however, did not change. A 1904 crazy quilt, an antique canoe on the wall, and a turn-of-the-century sleigh on display above the bed are just a few of the ways Patrice brings the cabin ethic inside.

Architectural iron purchased at a summertime antiques fair was a perfect fit for the windows in Pat Millington's ranch-house bathroom. The pieces hang from simple hooks embedded in the sashes. Pat rescued the tub from the dump in a small Idaho town and repainted it.

LEFT: Chink or caulk is sometimes used to cover imperfect seams between Sheetrock walls and logs. A length of rope works just as well and is usually worth a second look.

"But no real collector . . . ever buys something because of what he is going to do with it. That's just shopping. Collecting, on the other hand, is falling in love. And much more fun."

——*Louis Oliver Gropp, Editor-in-chief,* House Beautiful

Vertical stacks of log ends poking into the room are incorporated into the décor. While the owners could have trimmed them back, they had more fun saddling them up with ranch-house collectibles. A trio of rifles forms a base for an eccentric Wild West floor lamp, while an old piano brought out of retirement with a fine new coat of paint fits perfectly in the niche created by the log intrusion.

CABIN COLLECTIBLES

Despite being all grown up and perfectly capable of formal and sophisticated airs, there is no denying that log homes come from a long lineage of doin' and usin' stock. Pioneers and trappers, cowboys and Indians, even homegrown American presidents slept and supped in the humble shelter of logs. Today, we adore these notions and fancy that heroic, romantic life on the plains, on the range, and in the untrammeled wilds. What a case we make for furnishing our homes with the trappings of everyday stuff: the things people use, wear, and eat—or the things they used, wore, and ate. Tools, hides, heads, utensils, quilts, blankets, boots—logs make friends with them all. Fix it to the wall, saddle up a beam, or set a canoe afloat in the rafters. Pound a railroad spike into a log and hang your hat. Oops, too high? Yank it out and pound it in somewhere else.

Chasing down those cabin collectibles is, in itself, part of a home's own story and emerging history. From well-heeled galleries and festive fairs to the musty corners of failing barns, the search often becomes an adventure worthy of retelling. It is also part and parcel to an education that will turn your finds into personal treasures and favorite things. Earnest collectors revel in the history and authenticity of rare and unique vintage items, but you don't have to take yourself too seriously to get caught up in the spirit of the hunt and subsequent enjoyment of the booty.

You may already know what you like or you may need to spend some time refining your tastes. Resist the urge to get your cabin totally "done" before you move in. Snapping up a house full of newly purchased western accessories the same month you lay down the welcome mat may result in rooms that, while attractive, are neither familiar or personal. Chances are, you'll tire of them quickly.

There's no question that rare objects and well-preserved antiques can be expensive, but you need not be rich to seek out wonderful things.

Collecting, explains Alan Edison of American West Gallery, can be a very democratic thing unless, of course, you insist on the very best. An original 1930s couch by the famous western furniture maker Thomas C. Molesworth can fetch up to $35,000—that's if you can even find one. But there are other old pieces by lesser-known artisans and wonderful new spin-offs by contemporary craftsmen with approachable price tags. Folk art, windmill weights, old movie posters— such things can be found for hundreds of dollars (or less) or for thousands and thousands. It's more important to have a knowledgeable point of reference and a sense of what you like. Then save your

At Lonestar, shelves full of cabin accessories offer inspiration for your own homespun arrangements. Feel free to borrow ideas from all your favorite shops and haunts.

FACING PAGE: An eye-popping plate draws your gaze back to replicas of old gears on a table behind the couch. Arranged according to height and size, the gears are juxtaposed with other objects of varying shapes and textures. Architectural elements on the wall frame a leather-wrapped mirror.

"Home wasn't built in a day."

—Jane Sherwood Ace

A new birch-bark hutch at Lonestar is filled with a collection of brown-and-white transferware. Maybe some people wouldn't mix the Victorian china with a rustic hutch, but Terri likes the way it ties in with the colors of the cabinet. Besides that, oddball and unpredictable is fun. Objects are mixed according to height and layered with big things in back. A bowl of green apples adds an extra splash of color. It's a simple arrangement that isn't overdone.

money and buy the best that you can personally afford.

Experienced collectors also emphasize that you should always examine the things you buy. In the excitement of acquiring something neat, you can overlook important details that will impact value. Condition is everything. If mice have dined upon that great old saddle, even fifty bucks may be too much. Check for rips and stains, and ask about old repairs. Sit down in that chair and scoot around. Are those joints tight? You've heard it before. You've said it yourself. If it sounds too good to be true, that's because it probably is.

BUT dealers can't possibly know everything about the pieces they buy and sell. If you want to get lucky, you can help that luck along by knowing something about the items of your heart's desire along with the

acknowledged value in the marketplace. Then when you stumble on an undervalued find, don't gush. Put on your best poker face and offer a little less.

Books and shops, museums and fairs, manufacturers, auction houses, or a family-owned café in a one-horse town might all be sources of inspiration, information, and insight into the radically diverse realm of cabin collectibles. For a more serious study into the market value of virtually anything that tickles your fancy, Alan suggests you check the schedule of events at major auction houses. Upcoming sales on everything from folk art and western memorabilia to Navajo textiles and fine art are usually listed six to eight months in advance. You can purchase a catalog for one specific event, and the results of that auction will automatically be mailed to you whether you bid or not.

ARRANGING COLLECTIBLES

Perhaps it's true that some people are born with a knack for collecting, not to mention the gift for displaying and arranging their collections. Collecting, however, is not shopping. My husband loathes shopping, but he can sniff out an old sign or track down a vintage guitar with the best of 'em. As for arranging, well he doesn't sweat that part, but his sensibilities tend to junkyard casual, so he's easy to please. Good ideas, though, are everywhere, and you can learn as you go.

Designer Terri DeMun, owner of the popular home-furnishing store and design atelier Lonestar, recounts pleasurable weekends of collecting and exploring in laugh-out-loud stories. How about the time they sawed a bed in half to get it home, or the time she had to wear a

huge Chinese gardening hat on the commuter plane because it wouldn't fit in her bag. When the wind came up during boarding, it took half the passengers to keep her and the hat in the general vicinity of the airport. Then there was that joyful moment when she stumbled onto a $500 antique toy with a $20 price tag. Terri took it back to her own shop only to have one of the most respected women in American decorating walk in one day, look back and forth over her shoulder, then snatch it up with gusto.

While Terri may have been born a collector, the spirit is contagious. Buy what you love, says Terri, and take advantage of the labors of others. Anytime she sees a ready-made collection she adores, boom! She'll buy it. It may not matter that only one of the five

Roman-style frescoes, antique glass, and an extensive collection of ethnic jewelry make an intriguing but useful display. Artfully arranged on the dresser or hung simply from hooks pounded into pole window trim, pieces are easy to see and select.

A school of antique lures line up on a windowsill like fish hovering in a stream.

FACING PAGE: A hodge-podge of African and Native American art and collectibles are happily mixed up in this living room that pays tribute to the travels and life experiences of its owners. On the wall, a giant tapestry framed with logs serves as a major backdrop and directs the tone and color of the earthy space.

walking sticks is really great. Terri isn't purporting you buy junk, but groups of simple things have collective appeal. Besides, says Terri, you can worry less about the provenance of things as long as you aren't paying antiques prices. When Terri first started shopping, she couldn't afford the vintage blue-and-white china that she loved, so she made herself a deal. She would seek out wonderful pieces, but they had to be flawed and priced at next to nothing. Ten years later she had a chipped but stunning collection on display. What's more, each piece stirred the memory of a certain place or event.

Oftentimes, the way you arrange your things is as satisfying as what you're displaying. Try hanging up an odds-and-ends collection of paddles on a log wall, or run pairs of high-stylin' cowboy boots, weather-beaten birdhouses, or a line of colorful old tins up your stairs. Whether you're visiting a retail store or reading a magazine, examine any arrangement that

draws your eye, and borrow whatever strikes your fancy.

• Work with collections of similar or related items. Use five or six flowerpots instead of one great big one. While symmetrical arrangements are often pleasing, interweaving tall and short with skinny and fat makes a more interesting composition.

• Place the largest items first, then fill in the spaces around and in front of them. Play with your arrangements, taking time to step back and view them from afar.

• Stack items to create pleasing lines and shapes. Place a basket of spurs on top of a stack of books or a bowl of Rainier cherries on a pile of plates.

• Lean things against a wall—like plates and trays on a shelf, mirrors, or a collection of pictures on the mantel.

• Fill up baskets, crocks, or most any fun container with interesting or useful items and collectibles.

• Hang things on and over your logs.

From the 1930s to the 1960s, Gene Autry was "Public Cowboy #1," starring in western movies and a television series where the good guys still said "pardon me" before they threw a punch. Owners Ed and Shirley Cheramy met Gene in his later years and decked out their "cowboy bedroom" in his honor. They started with signed movie posters, then Shirley stumbled onto the original 1950s Gene Autry chenille spread at a western-collectibles show in California. Stenciled walls, a custom longhorn bed, and lamps made from six-shooters and a saddlebag add a little more giddyap to the room.

COLLECTING IN CYBERSPACE

The computer has wrangled its way into more American homes than fat-free salad dressing. It hasn't outpaced Coca-Cola or TV, but it may catch up soon enough. As for the home shopping channel—well, I've never gone there, but I have sat down to surf the net and check out some of the larger on-line auction houses. (Honest, I'm not a very savvy computer person, but after my friend Patrice Cole—she's not a computer person either—found a to-die-for weather vane for her chicken coop, the ideal hinges for her barn doors, and that 1930s stoneware bowl she'd been looking for, I had to take a peek.)

Wow! It's all there. I used www.eBay.com because it's currently one of the largest and most secure on-line auction houses on the Internet, but there are several others. You key in what you're looking for and bingo! You may find one or you

may find a thousand! If you're so in-clined, make a bid—much as you would at any auction. You'll have to monitor your bid, sometimes over a period of days. Then, if you're top dog, payment is arranged and the item is shipped your way.

We know, of course, or at least we hope and pray, that on-line shopping won't replace a leisurely foray to the country or an exhilarating pilgrimage from shop to shop where we can see and finger and sniff our way through piles of buried treasure. The Internet, however, can be another playing piece in that adventurous game we call collecting. Since there will usually be pictures,

dimensions, and a brief description of each item, you can merely use a site like eBay as a learning tool or to develop a point of reference on various items that you're searching for. However, if you plan to buy, don't assume that an item is original, old, or in perfect condition. If a skookum doll is only pictured from the front, ask about the back. Frequently, and if there is time to spare, you can contact the seller on-line to find out more. Be very leery about buying some-thing that doesn't have a seven-day money-back guarantee. I may be old-fashioned, but I still want to hold it in my hand.

The set of encyclope-dias shelved above the desk dates from 1892, the year Carol Gardner's log ranch house was originally built. When her son was in school, they had great fun comparing modern history with the knowl-edge and perspective of those former days.

An octagonal master bedroom is clothed in Victorian finery. Most of the furnishings are restored originals, including the Thomas Brooks bed and the inlaid music cabinet that dates from the 1860s. There will eventually be a painting above the marble-faced fireplace, but not until the owners can find one that is more beautiful than the wood!

ANOTHER MAN'S JUNK

*E*verybody recycles. Sometimes it may just be dinner from the night before or aluminum cans from the church picnic. Then again, it may be a light fixture devised from the grille of a 1930s truck or an entire house built with two-hundred-year-old logs. While the pickin's are getting slimmer, I still have friends who "shop" back alleyways and small-town dumps.

Recycling itself can be a form of art that interweaves the tracings of time with culture and, sometimes, wild imagination. Log-home buffs love that kind of thing because, in essence, the log cabin notion is recycled too.

Unlike collecting, recycling is more likely to combine function with intrigue. That's not to say that you won't put your collection of spongeware bowls to real use in the kitchen or enlist your silver candlesticks for their intended purpose, but when you set out to recycle old doorknobs, it may be because you really need doorknobs. Either that or you want

"If it isn't bolted down, bring it home."

——*Grace Murray Hopper*

This cabinet, originally designed to hold instruments and sheet music more than 130 years ago, was discovered by its owners on a visit to Antiquarian Traders in California. In the course of restoration, artisans at the store deepened the piece to hold a TV and added a remote-controlled lift.

to line three of them up on a paint-peeled board to make some kind of interesting but useful rack.

Since technology marches on, anything made well enough to outlive the inference of being in style may need a little updating to meet today's building or safety codes. Beautiful but inefficient old windows might be relegated to a sunroom that can be closed off in the dead of winter. You might also use them indoors or remove the glass altogether and conjure up an entirely new assignment for the sashes. Old cook stoves might need to be rewired or retrofitted with innards that will accommodate natural gas, and so on.

Giving an entirely new job description to some everyday or secondhand item is partly art, but it doesn't have to be a complicated affair. An old steamship trunk, Chinese laundry basket, or a wooden sleigh can stand in as a coffee table. A big ol' barrel topped with a round of heavy glass can seat four for cards or two for dinner. Fill those done-kicking cowboy boots with rocks and turn them into bookends. Anything can be used as a hook or hanger—from an old stirrup to a branched antler. Surely you've seen wagon wheels turned into chandeliers, and canoes with their bottoms lopped off standing upright and filled with shelves for books and collectibles. Apart from the bounds of common sense and safety, there really are no rules—only possibilities!

FACING PAGE: There are craftsmen who devote their lives to salvaging and restoring old log cabins. This home, built by Charles McRaven with now-extinct American chestnut logs, was originally built as a barn more than a hundred years ago. The floorboards and all the trim work are old too. The black spots in the wood are the trailings of nails removed before the boards were remilled.

ABOVE: Dump those drugstore boxes with their cutesy labels and repackage your bath salts, soaps, and powders in antique jars, boxes, and tins. Chuck the plastic garbage can for a galvanized bucket or old crock. For a total makeover, repaint your cabinetry and dresser drawers then add new hardware.

This old door sold out of a Sears Roebuck & Company catalog for $8. Pat Millington hauled it home from a wrecking yard in Denver—but that was nearly forty years ago. Doors like this can still be found, and if you snoop around grandma houses in small towns, you might get lucky. Other times, they'll just cost a little more! The glass in this door is new and was etched with the view that you can see from Pat's ranch.

This one-of-a-kind mirror frame is made from a collection of worn leather belts. The big silver buckles are gone, but nearly everyone who visits can still find their name tattooed on one of the straps.

This twin headboard is made from a door dating from the Spanish colonial period (1700s). Purchased from La Puerta in Santa Fe, New Mexico, you can still see the keyhole in the top right-hand corner. A casually draped serape adds a contrasting burst of color, and the bedside lamp plays into the lighthearted southwestern theme of the room.

FACING PAGE: In the master bedroom, recycled leaded-glass shutters fold open to view the great room below.

ABOVE: Barbed wire and a rusty roof turn this old boot into a fitting abode that would do any true western bird proud.

Steve and Cecilia Abbey's house was built in 1915 from a sawn-log kit. Steve bought the house and three acres of land for $30,000, then set himself to the task of fixing it up. Some items, like the kitchen appliances, were purchased from another home undergoing renovation. Wood, marble for the tub, windows, and countless other items came from the want ads, estate auctions, an old chicken coop, and even the dump. Today, after a whole lot of sweat equity and $15,000 extra dollars, his house has been appraised at five times that initial investment.

NEW LIFE, NEW LIGHT

"Sockets and wires"—whether you're making a lamp out of a pile of antlers or a rusty teapot, that's all you really need, say the experts. In fact, with a little imagination, just about anything goes. Yes, there are lighting codes and, in many fixtures, a high degree of artistry, but the parts are all standard and the technology quite basic. That's a big

whoopee for log-home owners who revel in fine antiques and plain ol' great junk.

An antique fishing creel, apothecary tin, or a birdhouse can serve as inspiration for a simple sconce or lamp assembly, but the demand for restored and rewired antiques keeps people like Mike Dalio of Light Years Antiques and Restoration busy plowing through seven barns full of old fixtures and parts. While

The sconces in this upscale Victorian bathroom are rewired elevator lights from a historic building in Chicago. They were once mounted on the outside of the door and originally had bulbs on the bottom as well as the top. You could tell which way your ride was going, depending on the end that was lit.

piece has historical significance. "Antique fixtures can be a very important part of your design." People like Mike can also help you track down hard-to-find period pieces. If you go that route, it's helpful to send your lighting specialist idea-pictures along with lighting criteria and snapshots of the house or room you want to accessorize.

Dating back to the 1890s, this Victorian-style fixture is from an era when electric lighting was hardly reliable. As a backup, household lights like these were both electric and gas burning. The upper lamps were fueled with gas while the lower ones ushered in the modern electric age. Steve Abbey's recycled fixture hangs from a ceiling covered in embossed wallpaper—the budget-wise equivalent of old tin. The paper is painted white to help lighten the room.

European fixtures can pose their own set of problems, Mike can restore, update, or often duplicate almost anything. That includes converting candle burners or kerosene lamps to electric lights, or parlaying one antique sconce into eight recast copies for a hallway or room.

The cost of updating old fixtures can vary widely depending on the condition of a piece and the degree of restoration or authenticity that's desired. If the update is simple and the lamp doesn't need to be reworked, it can be a bargain. Other times, you might pay more, particularly if you need to replace original globes and shades. Good reproduction parts, however, are often available and include new bulbs made from old molds.

Comparing the cost of old to new can be an apple-orange thing, says Mike, especially if you're after quality or the

TIP

The hunt for old lightbulbs can lead you down a dimly lit path unless you know where you're going. Martha Stewart promotes a few new-to-look-old styles that you can buy. For a much bigger selection of antique reproductions and hard-to-find bulbs, try a company like AAMSCO Lighting Inc. at www.aamsco.com. For candle covers, bulbs that mimic flaming candles, or actual electric, hand-dipped beeswax candles, visit Elcanco, Ltd., at www.elcanco.com.

ART WORKS!

RIGHT: The owners of this scribe-fit log home brought this contemporary oil with them from their former home. To their surprise, the painting actually appealed to them more in their new log home than it did in their smaller townhouse. What the painting needed was more room, and the bold colors played surprisingly well against the logs.

BELOW: Simple clips from an office-supply store make gentle hangers for this delightful hooked rug. A fascinating story inspires the imagination in this primitive piece of American folk art. A faux-wood frame is hooked around log cabins, a stone gristmill, and a plethora of activity. Other methods of securing wall hangings include the use of Velcro strips, quilt hangers, and rods slipped through sleeves sewn onto the back of a piece.

FACING PAGE: Alison Luckman uses a series of framed and matted prints to lighten and define the spaces in her tall ceiling. These wonderful prints were cut from a single book purchased at an antiques fair in Pennsylvania. In the foreground, a collection of kachina dolls dance their way across the tie log overhead.

*C*hunky, bumpy walls—log-home nemesis or serendipitous good luck? People who love art may gulp at the thought of hanging (or trying to hang) a piece of abstract art on a log wall. Tapestries and rugs . . . okay. Cowboys and Indians . . . fine. But how about something more contemporary?

Why not? is the answer most commonly echoed through the industry. If you love it, you can always make it work, says Char Thompson of Artigiano Creative Design. Of course, when building new, collectors will look ahead, strategically planning for framed walls in rooms or along extra-wide hallways. When it comes to the logs, they will also let their designers and builders know what they plan to hang and where. Large irregular logs can be the most troublesome, particularly if one willful trunk happens to stick farther out into a room or shows up with a particularly large and expressive knot smack-dab in the center of a major art wall. You can avoid that with a little on-site intervention when setting the logs. There are also chinking lines to consider and the fact that logs are often stacked at alternating heights around a room.

Flat logs or those that are uniformly sized and shaped may be less awkward, but I've yet to meet a log-home owner who was

"Art imitates Nature in this: not to dare is to dwindle."—John Updike

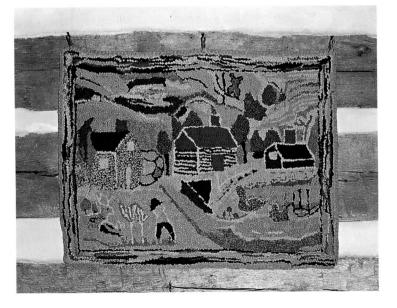

stopped cold by a few errant dips and humps. Instead, they will use corks behind their pictures to even out irregular spaces so a picture sits flat against the wall. Depending on the size of the logs and type of construction, settling might occur in a home's first few seasons of use. Art on the walls may need some minor adjustments over time. Sharon Henderson of Sage House uses crumpled tissue to temporarily help float groupings of pictures on a wall. Later on, she'll go back and make the fix more permanent.

Rather than denounce their logs, people love the freedom of pounding nails into less-refined wood. Logs are forgiving, and you can make plenty of mistakes without having to putty or repaint the wall. Small holes virtually disappear. That makes it easier to have fun with your art and move pieces around if you're so inclined.

Built by Alpine Log Homes and decorated more than ten years ago in subtle southwestern overtones, this log home was recently remodeled to liven up the spaces and augment the owners' substantial collection of French poster art. Interior designer Myra Prusky and the owners used a mixture of English and Islamic prints along with antique needlepoints that play off the artwork without overpowering it.

LEFT: A museum-quality collection of western and Native American art was an important consideration in the design of this home developed by its owners and architect Robert Gordon. The inclusion of plastered walls in the foyer and gallery-sized hallways ensured display space for weavings, artifacts, old photographs, and fine art. Extra ambient lighting prevented corners, high-trussed ceilings, and rooms full of log walls from appearing dark. A Frederick Remington bronze sculpture sits on a rotating pedestal in the center of the foyer. The chandelier was custom-designed by Peter Fillerup, and Roy and Robert Fisk crafted the mosaic door. Each artful piece is part of a collective story about the house, the art, and the family who built it. Oregon Log Homes and Dembergh Construction are the builders.

The owner wanted a tree in her bedroom, and craftsman Glen Carter threw in the beaver for good measure. The bed is built high to make room for storage underneath, and to give the owners a better view of the real beaver, deer, and elk that frequent their riverfront yard down below.

FACING PAGE: Rich but rustic retreats hidden away in the Adirondack Mountains in New York State defined a campy style that has contributed to cabin lore since its inception. Parented by developer William West Durant at the turn of the nineteenth century, these Adirondack havens were characterized by respectable craftsmanship and the use of natural materials—primarily birch-bark papering, twigs, rocks, and logs. The skilled and unskilled alike could rusticize anything from chairs and stairs to a fireplace like the one pictured here.

"Rustic: Appropriate to the country and using materials as found in nature."—Harvey Kaiser, author

RUSTIC FURNITURE— WHIMSICAL WOOD

The advent of crude log-and-pole furniture may have largely been a practical matter for wilderness-bound people needing a table and chair, but what happened next was as predictable as spring bloom. Link the human touch with the provocative and expressive natural world and you've got delightful, whimsical, functional art!

While the history of rustic furniture is in tangles reaching back through the ages, a sort of creative rebellion marked its passage through the western world and onto American shores. In a rebuff to stuffy Victorian protocol, landscape architects placed rambling arbors and twiggy benches in traditional European gardens. "Lighten up!" was the word on the cobbled streets. Justly inspired, America was quick to follow suit with

woodsy works that sprouted up in New York City's Central Park and other famous public places.

Soon thereafter, wealthy Americans adopted the rustic look in eastern Adirondack retreats and civilized western dude-ranches-turned-tourist resorts. Characterized by the use of twigs, birch-bark papering, roots, burls, and horns, rustic furniture became synonymous with Adirondack style, the western cowboy mystique, and other romantic notions of pioneers, independent thinkers, and the log-cabin lifestyle.

Having said that, today's artisans are certainly not contained by those historic prototypes. Rustic furniture can be built with any wood from any forest around the world with unique and varying results. And while we tend to think of rustic pieces as being sturdy, functional, and casual, they can also be free-flowing, refined, and even delicate. What's more, the furniture isn't confined to cabins and lodges any more than it is to tables and chairs. "Rustic" can conjure nature's fragrance in city homes and country cottages alike—or be expressed in a million ways, from a drawer pull or a picture frame to a horseshoe-handled country log casket!

LEFT: Pliant and supple, fresh willow boughs can be shaped, braided, curved, and swirled into any number of free-flowing designs. The addition of paints and dyes can soften the rustic edge and change the entire look and feel of the furnishing.

Stephen McAulay started making simple willow furniture, then he got ambitious. Wanting to branch out, he began to experiment with birch-bark papering and other materials. These dressing-room bureaus were two of those early pieces. Willow mosaics and trim work decorate drawers lined with aromatic cedar. There are deer-antler pulls down below and an entire elk rack on top that supports an attached mirror and doubles as a hat hanger.

The Reverend Ben Davis was a travelling Southern Baptist preacher in the early 1900s. In exchange for room and board, he often left a family with a handsome piece of furniture. Today his sense of rustic style lives on. Doug Tedrow was commissioned to build this Ben Davis knockoff using an elaborate design with pieces of notched willow over a birch veneer. While this piece is intended as a wardrobe for clothing, similar pieces make wonderful entertainment centers.

TIP

Meet rustic crafters and see their wares at design shows around the country. For the best in the West, show up in Cody, Wyoming, for the annual Western Design Conference held the third weekend in September— www.westd.org. Want more? Head east for the Adirondack Museum Rustic Furniture Fair, which is also held every September—www.adkmuseum.org.

*"I'd rather have roses on my table
than diamonds on my neck."—Emma Goldman*

BRINGING NATURE IN

*L*ife is full to the brim. We sprint from the house to the car to the office to the store to the school to the gym to the house. Sometimes we run so fast, we don't see the forest *or* the trees, yet we long for their presence in our lives. That's partly why we look to logs. If we can wrap nature around us, we feel calmer and more grounded.

Sometimes our need for nature is as basic as our thirst for water, and bringing nature inside is partly instinct. One day you may look at your art, fabric, and furniture and realize that you've done it without thinking. Other times, people deliberately look to the willows, the woods, or the distant red-rock cliffs for their colors and inspiration.

Patti Bosket of Au Naturél specializes in the simple art of using nature's gifts to create harmony inside a home. She comes by some of her most beautiful accessories on visits to nearby fields and forests. Urns full of long-lasting corkscrew willow, red dogwood, and paper birch are easy ways to impart nature's signature inside. Baskets and containers full of earthy collectibles and fresh flowers make a home feel lived in and comfortable.

In the sage-anchored hills and finger canyons reaching throughout southern Idaho, you'd think the wind would wear itself out—but it doesn't. Running short on patience, the owners of Suzie Q Ranch enclosed their back patio and turned it into a solarium and room for the hot tub. They removed the glass in the living room wall but left the opening. Initially, they worried that the house might smell like a public pool, but they don't use too many chemicals and it's never been a problem.

This wood-burning cook stove was included with the sale of this little cabin. Although it was in working order, the homeowners purchased an updated model for cooking and baking. Now, they use this stove for storage and for vibrant displays of seasonal fruits, vegetables, and fresh-cut flowers from the garden.

· Every home should have a comfortable corner for restful retreat. A
· warm bath with a tranquil view can be as soothing as a summertime
· nap under a shady tree. Fragrant candles, natural sponges, and
· baskets of handmade soaps and raffia-tied cloths soothe weary senses.
·
· RIGHT: The scents and sights of nature overflow in this combined
· dining/living area built by Timberline Corporation and Custom Log
· Homes. Greenery spills from a planter (complete with an indoor
· sprinkler system) set into a log rafter overhead. Wicker, a swinging
· hammock, fresh floral stencils, and plants and flowers galore bring
· summer inside.

Press dried flowers and frame them or use them between glass panes in the doors of your kitchen cabinets. Tuck bird nests here and there among your logs or on your shelves. Participate in the gathering and involve your children in appreciating some of life's truly simple pleasures.

Imminently changeable, nature itself shows us how to use and enjoy color and variety. New bounty flows from season to season, and we can take our cue from spring blooms, summer fruits, fall harvests, or winter cones and berries. When long warm days prevail, transform a room with bright floral slipcovers on the sofa. In the fall, replace the bed's cool cotton quilt with a downy duvet, darker linens, pillows, and snuggly flannels. Change table linens, draperies, blanket throws, or art on your walls to suit seasonal shifts and moods.

STONE SOUP

- Make place cards by writing your guests' names on stones.
- Place stones in bowls or jars of fresh water for a colorful display.
- Use stones to make a changeable pattern or picture on a tabletop.
- Have your home address engraved on a boulder in the yard or a flat stone for your wall.
- Make quick paperweights, doorstops, and bookends with plain or painted rocks.
- Work small stones into the chink lines of a room for a playful rustic look.
- Warm a flat stone in the oven and place it in the bottom of a bread basket.
- Bring home memories in stones picked up on your travels.

This tiny mountain cabin was claustrophobic and dark, while a beautiful emerald forest waited just outside the door. That all changed with the addition of this spacious add-on sunroom that virtually puts the room in the forest and the forest in the room! When the darkest days of winter make this glass-filled space difficult to heat, it can be closed off from the rest of the house. For the enjoyment of all, a bowl of family photos sits on the table.

"Simple pleasures are the last refuge of the complex."—Oscar Wilde

BRANCH OUT!

Use twiglets, branches, or sturdy limbs to:

- Fashion hooks and hangers, door and drawer pulls.
- Make curtain rods—use wrought-iron rings for hanging since they'll slide over the branch better than wood rings will.
- Fill vases and urns or embellish a grocery-store bouquet.
- Clip a vase full of yet-to-bud twigs in the spring, water them, and see what happens!
- Make an Easter tree in spring or fill an empty flower box with evergreen boughs or berried branches in winter.
- Cut down a manageable white-barked birch or aspen tree after the leaves have fallen, then anchor it in a large stone-filled container in your home for dramatic and long-lasting natural beauty.
- Use a prominent stack of white-barked wood to fill in a black-holed hearth when the weather turns warm.
- Bind a small bundle of twigs with copper wire or twine and use at place settings or as a decorative touch on a table or shelf.

Nature is an open shop stocked to the brim with beautiful and free accessories for any home. Fill your baskets and bowls full of stones, shells, feathers, pinecones, or rose petals. Keep your clippers in the car and be on the lookout for dried grasses, clippings, and plants that you can whisk away. A big bunch of pussy willows will last a long time. When they get dusty, take them outside and blow them off. When they turn brittle, throw them away and find something new to take their place. In this home, an antique paisley shawl draped over a round of inexpensive plywood makes a beautiful station for nature's bounty. A line of bird prints over the dining room table also sings outdoor praises.

Accessorize!
picnic baskets •
fishing creels •
duck decoys •
snow shoes • paddles •
driftwood • seashells •
watering cans •
moss-covered pots •
botanical prints •
horse tack • bleached
skulls • garden wicker
and wrought iron •
old-fashioned fruit
and vegetable crates •
glass-topped
lobster traps •
hanging bunches of
dried flowers
and herbs •
stencils of vines
and flowers •
log-stump stools

A seasoned cutting board tops an old piece of furniture converted into kitchen cabinetry. Sugar and flour are stored away in antique crocks, and tonight's dinner is on display along with a pewter pitcher full of dry branches.

GET OUT(SIDE)!

A good many log-home owners are plain and simple, the outdoor kind. For one thing, they tend to build their homes at the end of the road or as close to it as they can get. They'll go to great lengths to save their trees—even if it means zigzagging decks around them or allowing trunks to grow up through the middle. They like to fish and hike or just watch nature happen out their windows. They'll even put up with deer in the garden, black bears poking around their backdoors, and moose trekking across their lawns. (I happen to know that because we've spent a good deal of time waiting for those unscripted wild creatures to wander into our photographs or, just as often, to wander out! They don't always sit still and tend to park themselves in distracting places or positions!)

Outdoor spaces enlarge living areas in due season and are often an extension of what log-home owners naturally value and delight in. Covered porches are good design since they protect log walls from adverse weather. Fill them with porch swings and rockers, line the walls with pegs for gear, screen them in, or even include an outdoor hearth. Send

In the midst of building, the owners realized just how abundant the mosquitoes were on their streamside property. That's when they decided to screen in the covered porch outside their kitchen. They even added heating elements in the ceiling to make the space a comfortable retreat from the first blooms of spring through the frosty fall.

stone-lined paths down to the brook or out to a hammock anchored under shady boughs. Then decorate! Western memorabilia and abandoned farm equipment make fabulous yard art. Collectible metal signs color-up a barn or a shed. Plant flowers and herbs in barrels and boxes, washtubs, and potbellied stoves.

Augment your existing vegetation with trees, shrubs, and flowering plants that are prolific, hardy, and native to the area. While the principles of good gardening apply equally to log homes, take extra care not to water your walls when you sprinkle your garden. By the same token, clinging vines or tall dense shrubbery that hug a house can hold excess moisture against the logs and cause premature aging and deterioration of the wood. And it's also harder to re-oil or re-chink walls where this kind of vegetation persists.

Large or small, decks, patios, and garden spaces can be your door into another world. Make them personal, keep them manageable, and they'll be yours to enjoy year after year.

"Of all the wonders of nature, a tree in summer is perhaps the most remarkable, with the possible exception of a moose singing 'Embraceable You' in spats." —Woody Allen

When Sherry Thorson first stood on this front porch, most of it wasn't here. The house, built in 1977, was the consummate fixer-upper. It didn't matter to Sherry. She liked what she saw and, better yet, what she smelled: the fragrance of redwood, damp leaves, and Girl Scout camp wafting up through the boards of the porch. When she bought the house, she added sixteen feet of new deck—enough for line dancing and country swing. Then she filled the space with ice-cream parlor chairs, old watering tins, a porch swing, and plenty of rockers that she and all her girlfriends can grow old together in.

A sign made with letters cut from rusty iron welcomes family and friends, while a new path made from stones pulled out of the front entry during a remodel meanders through a flea-market gate to the backyard. Rows of cosmos, daisies, and wildflowers cheer on the path and celebrate the peak of summer.

BELOW: Decks are synonymous with outdoor dining. Fresh flowers, a red-checked cloth, and garden-matched dishes set a pretty table on a deck overlooking the river. Remember that the setting summer sun can be intense, so plan for shade where necessary.

ABOVE: Shaped concrete mimics huge, river-polished stones in this patio and pathway leading to a stream-side deck.

How many lifetime memories are made around the campfire! Gooey s'mores, scary stories, and summer camp were just the beginning. This backyard deck recaptures the "remember whens" and clears the way for plenty more. Out of view, a footbridge crosses a gentle stream to a life-size tepee tucked back in the woods.

LANDSCAPE ARCHITECT

Landscape architecture goes way beyond flowers, shrubs, and trees, even beyond the decks, patios, and garden nooks included outside our homes. Landscape architects frequently work alongside home designers to help orient a home and develop the site. They will conduct solar studies, work out drainage issues, and design roads. Beyond that, both landscape architects and designers will help you create pleasing, well-lit outdoor living spaces, orchestrate garden paths, and coordinate beautiful displays of green and growing things. A good designer will also help you take optimal advantage of the existing foliage around your home and the natural contour of the site.

Old farm equipment is still plentiful and affordable in western states. Expired plows, retired tractors, and other abandoned farm memorabilia can dude-up any yard. This metal-bottomed manure spreader now brims over with summer blooms. A line tied into the sprinkler system takes care of the watering. The house address is painted on the side of the wagon, and a spotlight anchored in the grass kicks on at night.

RIGHT: Chain saw bears carved from big hunks of solid wood roam many a log-home backyard. This one is clamoring over the rail after a butterfly, while some of his friends are hanging from the second-floor deck and peeking into the children's bedroom windows.

In western states, seas of bleating sheep are still herded on horseback between mountain pastures in the summer and lowland farms in the winter. Likewise, sheepherders still summer with their flocks in covered wagons decked out for mountain living. Restored and often updated, these wagons are livable western treasures. This wagon, meticulously restored by Jay Bailet, was a chuck wagon, or movable cook shack. Now it's a one-room house complete with heat, water, and electric lights garnered from the renowned Orient Express based in Paris.

ROOM FOR *Improvement*

Tucked away in Idaho's Sawtooth Mountains, Busterback Ranch is a little piece of heaven (although the original owners first called it "Bust-yer-back" Ranch because they spent more time clearing rocks out of the pasture than lounging on the decks). When a new family moved in several years ago, they undertook a major remodel to open a series of small, compartmentalized spaces. In the kitchen, three rooms became one, making way for a new brick fireplace, a bay window behind the sink, and a work island big enough to crank out hearty fare for huge family gatherings.

*H*ouses grow a little like people do. They get older. Styles change. Eventually they may need a bit of cosmetic surgery—other times, it might be a heart transplant. If you've got an aging log house and a growing family, the time might be right to add on a new rec room or an extra bedroom. An older, nothin'-special house might need a decorative infusion of cabin spirit and some log accents to perk it up. Then there's the total fixer-upper. It may take a bone-crunching renovation and months of tender loving care to make it a gratifying family dwelling—but "make it" you can!

REDO IT!

*B*uilding from scratch is not for everyone. New custom log homes with all the trimmings can be expensive, sometimes costing as much as 10 to 30 percent more to build than comparable frame homes. The good news is, log homes tend to hold their value or even appreciate more over time than other forms of construction, so a well-built home is a good investment.

When the owners bought their little cabin by the river, it was furnished with futons, filled with cat litter, and had a beach towel for a bathroom door. Along with a thorough cleaning, they made some small structural adjustments, including the addition of a small cold entry in front. When the doorway was cut into the existing wall, pink fiberglass insulation spilled out of the new wounds. Contractor Bob Zuck patched up the logs with a row of diamond-shaped plugs. Handcrafted furnishings and a table lamp made from a pair of beaded deerskin leggings contribute to the wild and whimsical look inside.

"There's always room for improvement— it's the biggest room in the house." —Louise Heath Leber

Peeled poles used for wainscoting "log up" framed walls in this second-story bedroom. This particular treatment is a trademark of Peak Builders, and it warms the room. Turquoise and other bold colors used in the décor were inspired from handblown glass sconces on the walls.

FACING PAGE: Logs don't have to be structural to make an impression. In fact, many times they are incorporated into a home purely for aesthetics. In this case, log ends protruding through the stucco are short sections added merely for show.

Rustic half-lap siding and mortar chinking cover up framed walls in this ski town makeover by Design Coalition. Finished to the T with cowboy texture and color, this faux cabin feels like a true-blue log home.

Log railings can comple-ment many a house, adding a touch of rustic where perhaps none existed before. On this second-floor balcony, a sunburst rail is an artful touch, whether viewed from inside or out.

TIP

There are a number of companies that specialize in log maintenance and restoration and sell the products that you need to protect and beautify your home. For products, books, tips, and reference materials on everything from bug control to power-washing your logs, visit Schroeder Log Supply at www.loghelp.com. For an on-site consultation, inspection, or survey of your log-home restoration, maintenance, or service needs, try Woodstock Log Home Services at www.woodstocklog.com.

Sometimes your options to buy might be limited by your location. Land may be too expensive or not available in the area you want to live. Other times, families won't have the money or the stamina to build new. That's not to say that a major remodel will be a bargain. In fact, if you really go to town, you can actually end up spending as much as you would for new construction (and talk about stamina—think twice before you live in the midst of a remodel. It can be grueling). If you're really trying to save money or minimize stress, look to homes requiring less struc-tural modification or to dwellings that can be tackled one room at a time.

Beware—remodels are a breed of their own. They don't always respect your well-laid plans. Forrest Gump would liken them to a box of chocolates—you never know what you're going to get. Before you purchase an older log home, have it inspected by a builder in the know. Rotten logs can be replaced, but mitigating extensive dry rot can be a costly undertak-ing. Tying new logs into old can also be a little hairy depending on your approach. Before you buy an aging home, consider what you plan to do and seek advice. Then stay flexible and be ready for a surprise or two along the way.

Rough-peeled bunks introduce remnants of summer camp into this child's bedroom. Built right into the wall, they take the shine off both framed and smooth-sawn log walls.

Like so many families, John and Beverly Shaw bought their existing log house because they loved the general location and the two-and-one-half-acre site. The house left a thing or two to be desired, but nothing that an add-on and makeover couldn't fix. Among the changes was the addition of this large master suite. Wanting to introduce color and the Victorian flair from their former antebellum home in Tennessee, they chose log accents over stacked log walls (log siding was used on the exterior to blend with the existing structure). The fireplace is faced with manufactured stone. Their bed, built in 1855 before bigger was better, has been artfully enlarged to accommodate a king-size mattress.

TIP

Synthetic Stone They can make just about anything these days, including stone. Manufactured stone is lightweight, comes in a variety of styles, and usually goes up in less time than regular rock, so it often saves you money. True rock is extremely heavy and requires a full masonry foundation to support its weight, but synthetic stone can be applied to a wooden frame or used on a second-story fireplace insert without additional support from below. That makes it ideal for remodels and second thoughts. For information and an eyeful, visit the web site www.culturedstone.com.

MORE ROOM AT ELK CAMP

$\mathcal{D}$ick and Betty Smith built their conventional family home back in 1965. Remodeling that house has nearly become a hobby, says Dick. Now, more than thirty-five years later, the place has changed as much as their grown kids. Dick loves that kind of thing, though, so the thought of a major log remodel was something to relish. While Dick grabbed his sketchpad and donned his tool belt, he primarily relied on architect Mike Doty along with Peter Dembergh's talented crew of local craftsmen to double the size of the family's newly purchased log house near Sun Valley, Idaho.

Originally, the house was constructed with round logs. Wanting a different look, the family considered flat logs instead. As it turned out, that concept simpli-fied the task ahead. They framed the addition, then covered it with wain-board siding. When used on the wall and chinked, these thick sawn slabs resemble whole two-sided logs. On the inside, while they left some of the existing round log walls as is, they covered others with the same siding. "When you move closets, eliminate a fireplace, or take out existing cabinetry," says the architect, "you can end up with Swiss cheese. The scarring of the logs can be ugly." Sometimes those logs can be repaired or even replaced, but this time, siding them over made more sense.

The project went smoothly but not without the occasional spur-of-the-moment modification to the plan. Ideas just happened, and though Dick couldn't always be on the job site, he was comfortable enough with the crew to approve most of their innovations over the phone. The project took the better part of a year—but no, it's not finished yet, and knowing Dick, just maybe . . . it never will be!

The original living room didn't extend much beyond the dining room table. During the remodel, that gabled space was extended out more than twenty feet and filled with windows. While the walls are framed and sided with wain board, imposing round-log trusses reinforce the powerful illusion of a solid-log building.

The latticework of logs over the new kitchen was part of the old ceiling. While the architect raised the roof over the enlarged living space, he modified some of that existing log work and kept it low—both to create intimacy in the kitchen and to provide a framework for the lighting. The round-log wall at the back of the room was left intact, and a built-in cabinet fills in a gap that once served as the home's front entry. The cabinet is only ten inches deep, but they didn't want to side over the opening, and it was a simpler solution than trying to piece in new logs and match them to the old.

Old houses mended, cost little less than new before they're ended.

—Colley Cibber, 1700s

The master bedroom stayed much as it was with a few exceptions. A closet was removed and the round-log walls were sided over with wain board to hide gashes left in the wood. The deck was also extended and the windows enlarged to accommodate the view. Adding or enlarging windows can be a simple matter in a log wall as long as you don't remove too much of the wood. In this case, the existing logs were able to support the revised window scheme with only minor reinforcement.

RIGHT: A wine pantry and service bar is tucked away in a little alcove that opens off the dining room. This is one of those spur-of-the-moment modifications that took root while the remodel was underway. More room and the addition of a sink and refrigerator gave the pantry a multipurpose twist.

LIGHTEN 'EM!

*T*here it is! You've searched hill and dale for months looking for a log house that calls your name and fits your budget. There's only one problem: it's dark inside. What can you do? While there are a variety of structural and aesthetic solutions, the greater challenge lies in trying to lighten the logs themselves.

Unfinished logs that have simply grayed over time can often be lightened with solutions of bleach and water or some other weathered wood restorer. These products are usually applied under low pressure with a hand-operated agricultural sprayer. The chemicals have to be flushed away with a thorough fresh-water rinse, so a simple wipe-down won't do. This can be a soggy undertaking that is most practical on outside walls or inside a house that is being completely stripped and gutted down to the finished floors.

Dark stains will need to be chemically stripped or blasted away with water, sand, or some other material—usually applied under extreme pressure. Chemicals used to strip away paints and stains can be highly toxic, and their use is tightly regulated by environmental protection agencies. For instance, it may not be an approved option for a lake or streamside home. As with other chemical applications, the solution has to be rinsed from the logs.

Water- or sandblasting literally peels away the outer surface of the wood. The material is applied with a wand in a narrow but high-pressure stream directed at the logs. Either of these methods is faster than chemical stripping and is

generally nontoxic. Water, however, is wet, and sand is messy. If you've ever tried to clean up a toddler after a day at the beach, you have a vague idea of where that sand will go. Crushed corn, baking soda, steel slag, walnut shells, and even bits and pieces of sponge are sometimes used as an alternative to sand, depending on the condition of the wood, the ultimate objective, and the homeowner's budget. Some of these materials are less abrasive than sand, biodegradable, and easier to clean up. They can, however, require special equipment and be more costly or even unavailable in a given area.

When log-home contractor Dave Carter wanted to lighten the walls inside his own home, he covered them with a layer of plaster. For effect, he left small sections of the wall and some of the log ends exposed.

Hand sanding or grinding the finish off the logs is yet another option. This is a labor-intensive way to go and you might not want to hand-sand an entire house, but restoration specialists often use this technique for a small area or in combination with other treatments.

If the means to lighter logs seem drastic or impractical, consider some of the alternatives:

•   Lighten or refresh the color of your chink with something appropriately named "chink paint." It is available in a variety of standard colors but can also be custom tinted to suit your particular tastes. Because the paint is thick and opaque, a lighter color will cover a darker one with only one coat.

•   Paint the decking on your ceiling white or cover it with light-colored bamboo matting, soft suede hides, tin ceiling tiles, or even embossed (and possibly painted) wallpaper.

•   Plaster over one or two of your log walls, allowing bits of logs or log ends to show through.

•   Lighten up your window dressings, install bright fabric-covered valances, or affix large white shutters alongside the windows inside your house.

•   Use art and wall décor. Line up a row of prints framed with broad white mats, or hang up a quilt.

•   Install new carpet, or put light-colored slipcovers on your furniture along with armfuls of brightly colored pillows.

•   Enlarge an existing window. In log houses, it can be easier than you think.

Solid log walls make it difficult to conceal lighting that is added after the fact. Wires can be tucked behind chink lines if they're present, but sometimes, just getting the wires to the walls can pose a problem. When track lighting was added to the ceiling beams in this log dining room, the electricians simply ran the wires across the whitewashed decking to the fireplace and hid them behind the rocks. The wires on the ceiling were covered with a thin strip of insulating material and painted to match the wood decking. New rose-patterned carpet was chosen to brighten up the formal space.

LOGGING IT UP AT THE PUZZLEFACE RANCH

*B*uilt in the 1960s, chocolate-brown walls, dark shag carpeting, tacky furniture, not a log in sight—now, that, say David and Melinda Kornblum, is how

you describe an ugly house! Fighting off buyer's remorse, the couple and their daughter, AliRose, looked past the plain-framed ranch house to their site for comfort and reassurance. They had purchased the house because of the location—no neighbors, great views, and within the budget. Now all they had to do was turn that cow-hocked nag into something they could show.

The fireplace, says David, was the only interesting feature in the entire house. The mantel, however, is new and was purchased from the same fellow who hauled the burled porch posts out of the forest on horseback. This particular log, however, was a prize—fondly referred to as his pet log. When the ashes grow cold, a moose rack leans up against the fireplace doors. Elkhorn Designs in Jackson, Wyoming, made the rawhide tepee chandelier hanging from the newly opened ceiling in the living room.

As you peer past fresh pine walls and new pole-trimmed windows, a porch full of burls and comfy willow furniture invites western hospitality. New log siding hides the fact that this home didn't have a log to its name before the remodel. Super-insulated and nearly bug-proof are among the rewards of log siding over frame-built walls.

They already had roomfuls of western memorabilia and a log-home fantasy to boot. They just needed to log their new place up. Working with Tom Stoner, a take-charge sort of contractor, they moved into phase one. There was no soup-to-nuts plan, and they weren't sure exactly how far they would go.

Phase I

The battle cry sounded something like "Goodbye, chocolate brown!" Out went the shag carpeting and in came the sandblaster. They restored the natural color of the pine walls and installed new sisal-toned carpet throughout most of the house. (They might have waited on the

carpet, but they intended to live in the house before it was fully finished.) They also did some serious tweaking in the living room. Technically speaking, the space had an open-beamed ceiling with exposed triangular trusses supporting the roof. The only problem was that when you looked up, you mostly noticed the bottom part of the truss or the two-by-eights that ran from wall to wall at normal ceiling height. If you tried to hang a chandelier from the peak of the ceiling, you would peer up at it through this skinny framework of dark brown boards.

They opened up the ceiling by removing those triangular trusses and replacing them with steel rafter beams

wrapped in wood. Good-looking, structural iron-collar ties completed the new design.

Somewhere in between the drawing board and shop-vacuuming the sawdust, Tom happened upon a truckload of burled pine logs for sale in a hotel parking lot. After one look, the family bought every one and had Tom swap out their existing porch posts with these quirky, Wild West mavericks.

Phase II

They hadn't planned to, but they did. They replaced every window in the house and trimmed them with peeled-pine poles. Next, they covered the entire exterior with log siding and chink. They gutted the kitchen then retrofitted lightweight, hollowed-out log beams onto the ceilings (bolted to boards accessed from the attic). The Kornblums spent three times their original estimate, while living

amongst the wood chips and sheetrock dust to help justify their revised budget. "We did everything moment to moment based on visceral feelings," says Melinda. "We couldn't just stop in the middle."

David, also known as "Buckaroo Dave," is a cowboy poet; Melinda saddles up as a citizen volunteer with Jackson's mounted-police unit in the summer. They have a cigar-store Indian in their dining room, a kid-size mechanical horse rescued from a dime-store parking lot, and a buffalo named Buffy over their mantel. Their house is kitsch and fun and grown-to-order—a little, or a lot, like themselves and their western Wyoming life!

Initially, the family wanted a stone fireplace in the master bedroom. They just didn't have room. The mason suggested stucco that could be shaped and squeezed into the corner. Indian skookum dolls sold as souvenirs on reservations in the 1920s and '30s line the rock-topped mantel. The bedroom walls are also covered with rough-peeled siding. Melinda made the simple curtains and tied them back with rope.

They started over in the kitchen, gutting it then moving a couple of walls to open the space. The restored antique stove replaced a hideous electric-pellet burner. A branched log in the ceiling, new floors, and a kitchen table plopped on a giant burl all speak to the casual rustic theme. The kitchen chairs came out of a Nebraska coffee shop in the 1940s, and the tabletop was built to match with the same brands stamped on the seat cushions.

Resource DIRECTORY

PAGE REFERENCES FOLLOW THE NAMES

KEY: T= TOP • B=BOTTOM

R=RIGHT • L=LEFT

Architects and Home Designers

Barlow, Jim (30, 39b, 48, 64)
PO Box 839
Wilson, WY 83014
(307) 733-7113

Berlin, Larry (11, 52)
PO Box 4119
Jackson, WY 83001
(307) 733-5697

Doty, Michael (165–168)
Michael Doty Associates Architects
PO Box 2792
Ketchum, ID 83340
(208) 726-4228
(208) 726-4188 fax
E-mail: mda@mda-arc.com

Gordon, Robert
(21, 55, 56, 73, 120, 122, 134)
PO Box 1450
Jackson, WY 83001
(307) 733-4081

Jarvis Group, The (5, 29, 31, 33, 35, 42, 44, 72t, 77, 80, 83, 98, 149)
Janet Jarvis
PO Box 626
Ketchum, ID 83340
(208) 726-4031
(208) 726-4097 fax
E-mail: janet@jarvis-group.com

McLaughlin and Associates
(93, 96, 97)
Jim McLaughlin
PO Box 479
Sun Valley, ID 83353
(208) 726-9392
Web site: www.mclaughlinarchitect.com

Neifert, Dennis W. (84)
PO Box 729
Sun Valley, ID 83353
(208) 726-3124
(208) 726-3517 fax
E-mail: dnaarchitect@sunvalley.net

Prestrud Architect, PC (14, 38, 41, 86, 102, 145)
Kristoffer Prestrud
PO Box 3624
Jackson, WY 83001
(307) 733-5391
(307) 733-2070 fax
E-mail: kris@prestrudarchitect.com

Pruitt, Steve (28, 156)
Architecture + Stephen Pruitt, AIA
PO Box 208
Sun Valley, ID 83353
(208) 726-3583
(208) 726-1856 fax
Web site: www.archplus-sv.com

Ruscitto/Latham/Blanton
(x, 2, 17, 46, 87, 92, 108)
Jim Ruscitto
PO Box 419
Ketchum, ID 83340
(208) 726-5608
(208) 726-1033 fax

Ryan, Michael (59, 65)
Michael Ryan Architects
60 Loveladies Harbor
Loveladies, NJ 08008
(609) 494-5000

Interior Decorators and Designers

Artigiano (25, 31, 71, 76, 98)
Char Thompson
PO Box 1741
Ketchum, ID 83340
(208) 788-4320

Au Naturél
Patti Bosket
11025 Eagle Creek Road
Leavenworth, WA 98826
(509) 548-4788
E-mail: PBosket@email.msn.com

Bennett, Barb (94)
Barbara K. Bennett Designs, Inc.
963 Buttrick SE
Ada, MI 49301
(616) 676-9972

Cowman, Beth (5, 33, 42, 77, 80, 140, 149)
Beth Cowman Interiors, I.I.D.A.
3921 NW Gordon Street
Portland, OR 97210
(503) 223-6594
(503) 226-1033 fax

**DeMun, Terri
and Lone Star Designs** (28, 67, 94, 113,
114–116, 125t, 144, 147, 156, 163)
Terri DeMun
PO Box 698
Hailey, ID 83333
(208) 788-9158
(208) 788-9170 fax
—A retail home-furnishings store with a
unique selection of one-of-a-kind and
antique home furnishings.

Design Coalition (161)
David Krajeski
PO Box 1180
Park City, UT 84060
(435) 649-6006
(435) 649-5648 fax
E-mail: david@paulpcdesign.com

e.k. Reedy Interiors, Inc. (102)
Kathy Reedy
PO Box 25167
Jackson, WY 83001
(307) 739-9121
(307) 734-9079 fax
E-mail: ekreedy@compuserve.com

Heminway, Hilary (16, 32b, 89)
140 Briarpatch Road
Stonington, CT 06378
(860) 535-3110
(860) 535-4546 fax
—Hilary also creates unique living areas
within restored sheep wagons. For more
information, contact Hilary
or Terry Baird at:
Montana Wagons
PO Box 1
McLeod, MT 59052
(406) 932-4350.

**Henderson Interior Design, Inc. and
The Sage House** (18, 26, 27)
Sharon Henderson
821 NW Wall Street
Bend, OR 97701
(541) 383-5006
E-mail: shdesign@hwy97.net
Web site: www.downtownbend.com
—The Sage House is a retail store
featuring unique custom furnishings and
any built-to-order piece that you can dream
up for your home.

Insights Interiors, Inc. (11, 52, 72b)
Liza Bryan
2316 Dellwood Drive
Atlanta, GA 30305
(404) 355-0282
(404) 355-6647 fax
E-mail: insights@bellsouth.net

Jenkins, Jacqueline (38, 41, 86, 158)
Inside Design
PO Box 13160
Jackson, WY 83002
(307) 733-2299
(307) 732-0421
E-mail: insidedesign@rmisp.com

Lucini, Elizabeth (x, 2, 92)
Elizabeth Lucini, Designer
2005 Branch Lane
Reno, NV 89509
(775) 827-1775

Martin, Bruce (94b, 147)
Interior Designer, Bruce Martin
PO Box 2860
Ketchum, ID 83340
(208) 726-4568
E-mail: bmartin@svidaho.net

Moreland, Susie (69)
By Design Interiors, Inc.
623 S. First
Hamilton, MT 59840
(406) 363-4473
(406) 363-1877 fax

Nicholson, Frank (87)
Frank Nicholson Incorporated
360 Massachusetts Avenue
Acton, MA 01720
(978) 369-0900
(978) 635-9979 fax
—Specializing in commercial
interior design.

Prusky, Myra (135)
MP Interiors Inc.
552 Sprague Road
Narberth, PA 19072
(610) 667-4275

Riley, Kathleen (3)
Kathleen Riley Interiors
2033 Claremont
Houston, TX 77019
(713) 621-6998

Rudigoz, Betsy (17, 46, 95, 108)
Candy Colored Dreams
PO Box 1992
Sun Valley, ID 83353
(208) 726-9727
or Seattle, WA
(206) 300-1774
E-mail: candycolors@dellnet.com

Ryan, Randee Spelkoman (59, 65)
60 Loveladies Harbor
Loveladies, NJ 08008
(609) 494-5000

Sagenkahn Designed Interiors
Chester Sagenkahn
7189 E. Genesee Street
Fayetteville, NY 13066
(315) 637-1860
(315) 637-4613 fax

Savoia-Shawback, Penny (37, 66)
Shawback Design Associates:
Interior Design • Feng Shui
PO Box 909
Sun Valley, ID 83353
(208) 788-4114 Idaho
(650) 369-4983 California

Schlapp, Patricia (7)
Earls and Schlapp, LLC
Interior Design Services
2800 - 60th Avenue SE
Mercer Island, WA 98040
(425) 743-9078
E-mail: jearls@home.com

Shepardson, Lori (93, 96, 97)
Northstar Design
PO Box 2242
Ketchum, ID 83340
(208) 726-4356
E-mail: lorishep@svidaho.net

Simpson, Kelly (50, 70, 75, 82, 104)
Design Line Interiors
28352 Via Mondano
San Juan Capistrano, CA 92675
(949) 487-3221
(949) 487-3224 fax

Slifer, Beth (29, 35, 72t, 83)
Slifer Designs, Inc.
PO Box 1409
Edwards, CO 81632
(970) 926-8200
(970) 926-8228 fax
E-mail: info@sliferdesigns.com
Web site: www.sliferdesigns.com

Sun Valley Kitchen and Bath
Lee Ann Ferris
PO Box 885
Ketchum, ID 83340
(208) 726-7546
(208) 726-7557 fax
E-mail: grferris007@aol.com

Wood, Andrea Lawrence (21, 55, 56, 73, 120, 122, 123, 130, 134)
Andrea Lawrence Wood Interior Design, Ltd.
1600 Wynkoop, Ste 100
Denver, CO 80202
(303) 893-3263
(303) 825-1948 fax
Web site: www.alwdesign.com

Artisans and Craftspeople

A Cut Above (94)
Tim Mylnar
22 Buttercup Road
Hailey, ID 83333
(208) 788-3108
—Specializing in all types of interior and exterior finishes for walls, floors, and cabinetry.

Adirondack Garden Rustic Furnishings
Drew W. Hubatsek
PO Box 8125
Big Fork, MT 59911
(406) 837-6868
—Creating a whimsical and relaxing environment for your home, cabin, or business.

Antiquarian Traders (123)
9031 W. Olympic Blvd
Beverly Hills, CA 90211
(310) 247-3900
Web site: www.antiquariantraders.com
—Specializing in museum-quality American nineteenth-century furniture, lighting, and architectural pieces, with more than 8,000 to choose from. Will also restore or modify furnishings and fixtures to order.

Armstrong, J. Chester (25)
PO Box 253
Sisters, OR 97759
(541) 549-9344
—Wood sculptor, primarily featuring Northwest American wildlife.

Bailet, Jay (155)
Jay Bailet Wood Working
146 Gannett Road
Bellevue, ID 83313
(208) 788-4077
—Custom furniture, sheepwagons, cabinetry, boat carpentry. He'll do anything in wood.

Bell Hardwood Floors (134)
325 N. Holmes
Idaho Falls, ID 83401
(800) 660-9694
—Specializing in custom hardwood floors and finishes.

Bordeleau, Jacques (37)
PO Box 3810
Ketchum, ID 83340
(208) 726-9241
—Fine stained and fused-glass art.

Buck's Masonry (173)
Buck Beckett
PO Box 1562
Jackson, WY 83001
(307) 733-4029
—Fireplaces for all your burning desires.

C.W. Pickets
Nance Shaeffle and
Estelline O'Hara
8102 SE Barbara Welch Road
Portland, OR 97236
(503) 760-2052
—Two old ladies (but not too old!) who design and create artistic and functional furniture using a blend of twigs, bark, and logs.

Carter, Glenn (136)
The Ketchum Zoo
PO Box 1715
Hailey, ID 83333
(208) 788-4113
Web site: www.ketchumzoo.com
—Makers of wonderful things.

Chase Construction (15)
PO Box 3910
Ketchum, ID 83340
(208) 788-2379
—Handcrafted log homes, unique railings, and furniture.

Cliffhangers Inc.
Jonathan Nasvik
PO Box 1466
Hailey, ID 83333
(208) 788-4196
—Specializing in imprinted and decorative concrete, including floors, counters, fireplaces, architectural pieces, and more.

Country Log Caskets
Patty Cramps and Kelly Miller
RR2
Pickardville, AB T0G 1W0
Canada
(780) 961-2334
—"Personal choice" for putting good old boys (and girls) in the ground.

Elkhorn Designs (171)
Richard and Kathy Keene
PO Box 7663
Jackson, WY 83002
(307) 733-4655
(307) 733-9200 fax
E-mail: cherokee@elkhorndesigns.com
Web site: www.elkhorndesigns.com
—Crafting of fine western furniture and fixtures.

Fillerup, Peter M. (134)
Wild West Designs, Inc.
PO Box 286
Heber City, UT 84032
(435) 654-4151
—Custom lighting, furnishings, hardware, and china.

Fisk, Roy and Robert B. (134)
PO Box 202
Bondurant, WY 82922
(307) 733-2822

Gem Painting (79b)
Karen Jones
PO Box 4899
Jackson, WY 83001
(307) 733-7209
—Painter specializing in a variety of unique and faux finishes.

Gladis, Ellen (79t, 104)
Ellen Gladis Originals
6208 W. Oceanfront
Newport Beach, CA 92663
(949) 645-0171
—Murals, trompe l'oeil, finishes, and custom fine art.

Golay Masonry
Byrd Golay
2140 Eldridge
Twin Falls, ID 83301
(208) 734-7728
—Quality custom masonry for more than 45 years.

Hink, R. C. (64)
PO Box 1142
Bellevue, ID 83313
(208) 788-6020
—Humorous, off-the-wall wood sculpture and furnishings.

Lamps by Hilliard (42)
Janene and Noel Hilliard
896 A Street
Arcata, CA 95521
(707) 826-1545
(707) 826-1561 fax
E-mail: lampster@humboldt1.com
—Makers of contemporary art-glass lamps.

Lei's Custom Tiles (96, 97)
Cliff Iverson
PO Box 1579
Hailey, ID 83333
(208) 788-3962
—Unique designs in tile, stone, and marble.

**Light Years Antiques
and Restorations**
Mike Dalio
Arvada, CO
(303) 422-4379
E-mail: lightyrs48@aol.com
—By appointment only. Specializing in antique and custom-built lighting for 28 years, with a large selection of 1870s to 1940s interior- and exterior-lighting products.

McCaulay, Stephen (139)
PO Box 363
Gaston, OR 97119
(503) 359-1000
—Fine rustic furniture.

Morgan's Fine Finishing (80)
PO Box 5266
Ketchum, ID 83340
(208) 726-6851
—Furniture-quality interior finishes.

Naos Forge (44)
1817 E. Avenue Q #C-15
Palmdale, CA 93550
(661) 273-5851
Web site: www.naosforge.com
—Designers of handmade wrought-iron furniture and lighting fixtures.

New West (39t, 81b)
Mike Patrick
2811 Big Horn Avenue
Cody, WY 82414
(307) 587-2839
(307) 527-7409 fax
Web site: www.newwest.com
—Distinctive contemporary and western furnishings.

Phred's Fabrication (108)
Donnie Smith
PO Box 3191
Ketchum, ID 83340
(208) 788-6334
—Specializing in ornamental and structural fabrication.

Pratt & Larson Tile (77)
1201 SE Third
Portland, OR 97214
(503) 231-9464
Web site: www.prattandlarson.com
—Innovative handcrafted ceramic tile, with more than 1,000 different designs.

Sheehan, Mark (109b)
Cherry-Glow Forge and Fabrication
PO Box 2386
Hailey, ID 83333
(208) 788-9475
—Mark is an artist-blacksmith whose decorative, architectural metal solutions cater to a discerning clientele who appreciate careful design, fine craftsmanship, and ease of function.

Stark, Paul (19)
Oregon Studios
PO Box 1381
Sisters, OR 97759
(541) 549-0136
(541) 549-4679 fax
E-mail: stark@outlawnet.com
or
New York Studios
151 W. Shore Road
Bethel, NY 12720
(914) 583-6500
—Specializing in dramatic wildlife wood sculpture in log homes, along with two- and three-dimensional pieces for any home or office.

Tedrow, Doug (23, 140)
Wood River Rustics
PO Box 3446
Ketchum, ID 83340
(208) 726-1442
(208) 726-1430 fax
—A designer and builder of rustic furniture in the old style and tradition.

Tribes (81t, 82)
711 N. Main Street
Ketchum, ID 83340
(208) 726-5003
or
203 5th Avenue South
Twin Falls, ID 83301
(208) 736-8990
—Offering design services and custom-made furnishings, primitives, tribal artifacts, and oriental rugs.

Vasileff, Gregory (32t)
797 Pomfret Road
Hampton, CT 06247
(860) 455-9939
(860) 455-9349 fax
E-mail: Gvasileff@snet.net
—Specializing in convincing antique-reproduction furniture.

Waterworks (98)
(800) 899-6757
Web site: www.waterworks.com
—Inventing kitchen and bath style with specialty tile. Call to order a catalog.

Ziniker, Robin (58)
Robin Ziniker Masonry Inc.
64870 Casa Court
Bend, OR 97701
(541) 382-0045
E-mail: zinn@bendnet.com
—Four generations of precision masonry.

Builders

A Place in the Sun Log Homes (84)
Gary Pendergrass
PO Box 6
Timber, OR 97144
(503) 324-8511
(503) 324-3712 fax
E-mail: loghomes@europa.com
Web site: www.theloghomestore.com

Adams, Ed (18, 26, 27, 29, 35, 57, 58, 72t, 83, 110br)
Handcrafted Log Homes
PO Box 625
Sisters, OR 97759
(541) 388-4602

Alexander, Ross (26, 27, 57, 58)
Ross Alexander Construction
20475 Woodside North Drive
Bend, OR 97702
(541) 382-8433

Alpine Log Homes (4, 59, 62, 63, 65, 135)
PO Box 85
Victor, MT 59875
(406) 642-3451
(406) 642-3242 fax
—Designers and builders of hand-crafted log homes.

Brian T. Smith Builders, Inc. (59, 65)
5700 Lower Mountain Road
New Hope, PA 18938
(215) 794-5193
(215) 794-2095 fax
E-mail: bsmith0531@aol.com

Carter, Dave (17, 28, 46, 156, 169)
Dave Carter Construction
PO Box 3360
Ketchum, ID 83340
(208) 726-7555
E-mail: davecarterco@sv.net

Custom Log Homes (159)
PO Box Drawer 226
3662 Hwy 93 North
Stevensville, MT 59870
(406) 777-5202

Davis Company, The (4)
715 W. Main Street, Ste 104
Aspen, CO 81611
(970) 925-9119
E-mail: DavisCoRe@aol.com
—Designer and builder of custom, handcrafted, full-round log homes.

Dembergh Construction Inc.
(21, 55, 56, 73, 122, 134, 165-168)
PO Box 3006
Ketchum, ID 83340
(208) 726-2440

Espe, Gary (22)
Norwegian Wood Log Homes
18920 River Road
Leavenworth, WA 98826
(509) 763-3675

Hearthstone Homes (9b)
120 Carriage Drive
Macon, GA 31210
(800) 247-4442
(912) 477-6535
(912) 477-6535 fax
E-mail:
hearthstonehomes@mindspring.com
Web site: www.hearthstonehomes.com

Hilgard Log Builders
Anderson, Blair
PO Box 891
West Yellowstone, MT 59758
(406) 646-7234

Logcrafters (101)
Stewart and Mary Thompson
PO Box 1540
Pinedale, WY 82941
(307) 367-2502
(307) 367-4475 fax
E-mail: logcraft@coffey.com
Web site: www.logcrafters.com

McNamara, Jack (20)
The McNamara Company
PO Box 1250
Sun Valley, ID 83353
(208) 726-2372
(208) 726-2559 fax

McRaven, Charles (13t, 124)
Charles McRaven Restorations
Drawer G
Free Union, VA 22940
(804) 973-4859

Miller, Ron (93, 96, 97)
Ron Miller Construction
PO Box 4762
Ketchum, ID 83340
(208) 788-3893

Montana Idaho Log Homes (x, 2)
1069 U.S. Hwy 93 North
Victor, MT 59875
(406) 961-3092
E-mail: info@mtidlog.com

Mutchler Construction (5, 33, 42, 149)
Wayne Mutchler
7306 NW Penridge Road
Portland, OR 97229
(503) 297-1139
(503) 297-7273 fax
E-mail: mutch5150@aol.com

Nash Construction, Inc. (6, 7)
PO Box 797
Ketchum, ID 83340
(208) 726-4646

Oregon Log Homes (19, 21, 55,
56, 73, 122, 134)
PO Box 1377
Sisters, OR 97759
(541) 549-9354
(541) 549-1135 fax
E-mail: business@oregonloghomes.com
Web site: www.oregonloghomes.com

Peak Builders, Inc. (38, 41, 86, 158)
John Jennings
PO Box 11007
Jackson, WY 83002
(307)733-9151
E-mail: peakcustomhome@cs.com

Pioneer Log Homes (5, 15, 33, 42, 149)
1344 Hwy 93
Victor, MT 59875
(406) 961-3273
Web site: www.rmlh.com
—The handcrafted division of Rocky
Mountain Log Homes.

Rea, Kevin (31, 98)
Kevin Rea Builder Corporation
1816 Maker Way
Bend, OR 97701
(541) 388-4121
(541) 385-8385
E-mail: kerea@empnet.com

Rocky Mountain Log Homes (68)
1833 Hwy 93 South
Hamilton, MT 59840
(406) 363-5680
(406) 363-2109 fax
E-mail: sales@rmlh.com
Web site: www.rmlh.com

**Sawtooth Wood Products
and Equipment Company** (6, 7)
PO Box 452
Bellevue, ID 83313
(208) 788-4705

**Spring Creek Timber
Construction** (3, 9t, 61)
Steve Cappellucci
635 County Road, #744
PO Box 429
Almont, CO 81210
(970) 641-3367

Staley Construction, Inc. (11, 39b, 48,
52, 64)
Hal Staley
PO Box 567
Jackson, WY 83001
(307) 690-0776

Stoner, Tom (24b, 171-174)
Tom Stoner Construction Craftsman, Inc.
PO Box 3287
Jackson, WY 83001
(307) 733-8075
(307) 733-8271 fax
E-mail: tomstoner@blissnet.com

Stopol, Richard (17, 46, 108)
Richard Stopol Log Homes
PO Box 1281
Hailey, ID 83333
(208) 788-9693

Sun Forest Construction (18, 29, 35, 44, 72t, 83)
Gary Bradshaw
PO Box 2378
Sun River, OR 97707
(541) 593-8204
(541) 593-6229
Web site: www.sforest.com

Timberline Corporation (145)
Fred Hibberd
400 NW Ridge Road
Jackson, WY 83001
(307) 733-7327

Unique Log and Timber Works, Inc. (8, 11, 30, 39b, 48, 52, 64, 87, 105)
Dave Gardner
1837 Shuswap Avenue
Lumby, BC V0E 2G0
Canada
(250) 547-2400
E-mail: info@uniquetimber.com
Web site: www.uniquetimber.com

Woodstock Log Home Services
10 Chenango Street
Cazenovia, NY 13035
(888) 483-5524
E-mail: woodstocklog@earthlink.net
Web site: www.woodstocklog.com

Woody's Log Homes (20, 34)
Art and Cindy Thiede
PO Box 2735
Hailey, ID 83333
(208) 788-4393
(208) 788-7619 fax
E-mail: thiede@sunvalley.net

Zuck, Robert (81b, 133, 157)
PO Box 1879
Hailey, ID 83333
(208) 788-9870

Home Systems

Audio Visual Design Group
Michael Clair
PO Box 3991
Hailey, ID 83333
(208) 578-0748
—One-stop super-shop installation and design firm.

Electronic Home Systems, Inc.
Joel Ranua
2495 E. Lenox Court
Eagle, ID 83616
(208) 938-2891
(208) 938-0555 fax
E-mail: lowvoltguy@aol.com
—Custom electronic systems for the home, including home theater, distributed audio, lighting control, and automation.

Spectrum Professional Services, Inc. (21, 55, 73, 120, 122,130, 134)
Glenn Johnson
175 S. Main Street, #300
Salt Lake City, UT 84111
(800) 678-7077
Web site: www.spdesign.com

Stoops, Paul
Paul Stoops Associates
PO Box 1130
Hailey, ID 83333
(208) 788-8993
(208) 788-8993 fax
E-mail: paulstoops@aol.com
—Architectural lighting and electrical design.

Wood River Custom Audio & Video
Eric Palmer
PO Box 2919
Sun Valley, ID 83353
(208) 726-5234
—A custom-consultation/installation company.

Home Products, Furnishings, and Accessories

American West Gallery (74)
Alan Edison
PO Box 3130
Ketchum, ID 83340
(208) 726-1333
—Fine and fun cowboy and Indian art and collectibles.

Charles Stuhlberg Furniture
PO Box 629
Sun Valley, ID 83353
(208) 726-4568
E-mail: stuhlberg@sunvalley.net
Web site: www.svliving.com/stuhlbergs

La Puerta (126b)
1302 Cerrilles Road
Santa Fe, NM 87501
(800) 984-8164
E-mail: lapuerta@lapuertainc.com
Web site: www.lapuertainc.com
—Showcasing the largest collection of antique doors in the world.

Period Lighting Fixtures
167 River Road
Clarksburg, MA 01247
(800) 828-6990
(413) 664-7141
E-mail: zoe@tiac.com
Web site: www.periodlighting.com
—Handmade reproductions of Early American lighting, 1620 to 1850.

Ralph Kylloe Rustic Design Gallery
PO Box 669
Lake George, NY 12845
(518) 696-4100
E-mail: rkylloe@capitol.net
Web site: www.ralphkylloe.com
—The country's largest gallery specializing in high-end rustic furnishings for the home.

Top Notch
Bret and Lori Berier
PO Box 2250
Ketchum, ID 83340
(208) 726-7797
—Interior design, space planning, fine
furnishings, and antiques.

Shows and Events

**The Adirondack Museum
Antiques Show**
—More than 100 dealers feature rustic
Adirondack furniture and accessories.

Held in conjunction with

**The Adirondack Museum Rustic
Furniture Makers Fair**
PO Box 99
Blue Mountain Lake, NY 12812
(518) 352-7311
E-mail: acarroll@adkmuseum.org
Web site: www.adkmuseum.org
—Held each September, the furniture fair
showcases one-of-a-kind hand-crafted
furnishings made from natural materials.

**America's Largest Antique
and Collectible Shows**
Palmer, Wirfs, and Associates
4001 NE Halsey
Portland, OR 97232
(503) 282-0877
E-mail: cpalmer@transport.com
Web site: www.palmerwirfs.com
—America's largest antique and collectible
shows, held three times annually. Contact
for further information.

**Old West Antique Show
and Auction**
PO Box 655
Cody, WY 82414
(307) 587-9014
(307) 587-5393 fax
E-mail: oldwest@cody.wtp.net
Web site: www.codyoldwest.com
—Held annually on the third weekend in
June. Featuring the finest in western
antiques, including cowboy collectibles and
Native American artifacts.

Western Design Conference
PO Box 1133
Cody, WY 82414
(888) 685-0574
(307) 587-1357
E-mail: info@westd.org
Web site: www.westd.org
—The nation's premier exhibition and
educational forum in western design. Held
annually in conjunction with the Buffalo
Bill Museum Art Show and Patron's Ball on
the third weekend in September.

Web Sites

Many of the web sites previously listed in
the text can only be contacted via the web.
They are not associated with companies or
individuals so we have not re-listed them
here. The following sites are associated
with people you can contact for more
information.

www.fauxlikeapro.com
—Learn about the different faux-finishing
techniques, purchase products, or find a
decorative painter near you. For more
information, call Sandra Kiss-London at
(888) 765-4950.

www.marthastewart.com
—Shop, browse, or gather fabulous
decorating and craft ideas to spice up your
home and garden for any occasion at any
time of year.

www.milkpaint.com
The Old Fashioned Milk Paint
      Company, Inc.
436 Main Street
Groton, MA 01450
(978) 448-6336
E-mail: anne@milkpaint.com
—Providers of old-fashioned milk-paint
products.

www.loghelp.com
Schroeder Log Supply
(800) 359-6614
E-mail: loghome@loghelp.com
—Specialty products for the log home.

www.traditionalbuilding.com
or
www.period-homes.com
—Your portal to the world of restoration,
renovation, and historical products for
residential and commercial construction.
Hundreds of links to suppliers of restoration and historical products and related
services. They also produce two magazines:
Clem Labine's Period Homes
and
Traditional Building
69A Seventh Avenue
Brooklyn, NY 11217
(718) 636-0788.

www.ultimatehometheater.com
Lutron Electronics
7200 Suter Road
Coopersburg, PA 18036
(610) 282-3800
E-mail: product@lutron.com
—Lutron Electronics has been a leader in
lighting control since 1961. Visit their web
site for advanced information on home
theaters and lighting-control systems.